THE IGNATIAN WORKOUT

the Ignatian workout

daily spiritual exercises for a healthy faith

TIM MULDOON

LOYOLA PRESS.
A JESUIT MINISTRY
Chicago

LOYOLA PRESS.
A JESUIT MINISTRY

3441 N. Ashland Avenue
Chicago, Illinois 60657
(800) 621-1008
www.loyolapress.com

Cover and interior design by Kathy Kikkert
Cover photo © Fogstock/Wonderfile

Library of Congress Cataloging-in-Publication Data
Muldoon, Tim.
 The Ignatian workout : daily spiritual exercises for a healthy faith /
Tim Muldoon.
  p. cm.
Includes bibliographical references (p. 187–189).
 ISBN-13: 978-0-8294-1979-5; ISBN 0-8294-1979-9
 1. Spiritual exercises. [1. Ignatius, of Loyola, Saint, 1491-1556.
Exercitia spiritualia.] I. Ignatius, of Loyola, Saint, 1491-1556.
Excercitia spiritualia. II. Title.
BX2179.L8M85 2004
248.3—dc22

                                          2003023189

Printed in the United States of America
08 09 10 11 12 13 14 Versa 14 13 12 11 10 9 8 7

contents

Part Two: Workouts

acknowledgments

IN REPRESENTING A CLASSIC WORK IN THE HISTORY OF CHRISTIAN
spirituality, I owe a debt of gratitude to many who have helped me to
understand it and put it into practice in my own life. First, to Iñigo
de Loyola and to those who have passed on his insights over the ages.
Second, to the Jesuits of Loyola Academy, Boston College, and
Campion Hall, Oxford, especially Mark Andrews, S.J., Joseph
Appleyard, S.J., Stan Fasci, S.J., Julio Giulietti, S.J., and Chris Boles,
S.J. Third, to the editors of *America* magazine, for their publication of
my article "Why Young Adults Need Ignatian Spirituality" (February
26, 2001), which started my thinking about how Ignatian spirituality
speaks to us today. Fourth, to Jim Manney of Loyola Press, who suggested that I turn the article into a book and whose encouragement in
the project I have greatly appreciated. Fifth, to Michael Sparough,
S.J., and Bill Creed, S.J., whose critical comments were especially
helpful. Finally, to Sr. Jeanne Marie Klisiewicz, whose direction has
helped me to understand what it means to be a person of prayer.

introduction

FOR MANY PEOPLE, THE COMING OF SUMMER IS A MIX OF EXHILARATION
and dread. It's exhilarating, of course, because it's the time for vacations, barbecues, visits to the beach, and long nights. But the down-
side is that suddenly people become preoccupied with having to get
into shape! I know that on the college campuses where I've been, the
gyms fill up sometime before spring break and stay that way until
classes end. Men and women flock to the treadmills, bicycles, weights,
and (my personal favorite) rowing machines, in the hope that they
can burn off the winter pounds and achieve the bodies that magazine
editors drool over. Every year I see this, and every year I wonder the
same thing: where have these people been over the winter? Maybe I
tend to be a little critical. But it seems to me that if someone is really
concerned with being fit, muscular, and svelte, that someone ought to
be at it year-round. Bottom line: you can't get a perfect body in one
fell swoop, no matter what the latest magazine headline tells you!

My experience as a college athlete helped me to learn something
about being in shape. I began rowing as a freshman, having had no
prior training, and it was a slow process. I remember watching the
Olympic rowers on TV and marveling at how incredible their skills
were. When I first got into a boat, I remember wanting to row fast

and hard, to feel the wind at my back as our crew cut smoothly through the river. The reality was that we splashed around like a bunch of uncoordinated children. That was the first lesson in patience. We all had to ditch our prior notions of how talented we were and get down to the business of learning slowly if we were ever to make progress. But gradually we did; and by the end of the season, though we were far from Olympic-level rowing, we were able to move a boat reasonably well—and it felt great. I still cherish the memory of that first feeling of rowing well; it was satisfying on a personal level because I had spent a great deal of time working on it. It was also just a lot of fun.

This book takes a look at the practice of spirituality in a way similar to getting in physical shape. We can learn a great deal about "spiritual fitness" from understanding physical fitness. Many people suffer from attitudes toward spirituality similar to their attitudes toward fitness, like those I described earlier: namely, wanting the results without really understanding the process that leads to results. We want to have inner peace, a sense of meaning, a connection to other people, a knowledge of God and the world—and we want it *now!* Sadly, too often this desire for spirituality happens in the wake of difficult times in people's lives. Some realize that something is missing, and so they go out looking for it in the hopes of making themselves feel better. But it doesn't work that way! Just because the warm weather is coming doesn't mean all of a sudden we can get into shape. Just because I see talented athletes doing their thing and I want to do it too doesn't all of a sudden make me a great athlete. And in the realm of spirituality, just because I want peace, meaning, and connectedness doesn't immediately make me a saint. All of these desires require a sense of reality, a sense that things take time, a sense that our work will pay off in the end.

So the first question we must ask if we are to get our spiritual lives in order is a basic one: What is spirituality? If I'm going to take a trip, I've got to know where I'm going. But in this case, the question is not so easy. There are so many different ways people out there use the word *spirituality* that it's hard to decide who's right. In this situation, then, we've got to use a little discernment. Whom can we trust? Let's eliminate the obvious: we can't trust only ourselves. For if we were so sure about what spirituality is, we wouldn't be asking questions about it. Unfortunately, a lot of people seem to think that spirituality is just about themselves—it becomes a "self-help" exercise, yet another kind of consumer product. If spirituality is to have any meaning at all, it must be about God. And when I use the word *God,* I don't mean that image that we all had as kids, of the old, old man with a long white beard and sunlight coming out from his head. Instead, I mean that spirituality is what leads us deeper and deeper into the mystery of life, of beauty, of truth, of goodness—in short, into the mystery of the person we name *God.* And since we can't trust only ourselves, we must trust those reliable guides who have, in their own lives, manifested beauty, truth, and goodness, and so are most likely able to show us how to move in the right direction. I am speaking about the saints: not the cardboard saints whose names people throw around like baseball cards, but those women and men who have with their very lives shown the very best of what it is to be human. In recent times, names like Mother Teresa and Cardinal Bernardin come to mind. In more distant memory are names like Francis of Assisi, Teresa of Ávila, Catherine of Siena, and Ignatius of Loyola.

All of the people I've mentioned have written on the spiritual life, and I am inclined to believe them simply because I want my life to be more like theirs. Mother Teresa, as many know, lived an unselfish life ministering to the sick and dying in Calcutta, India. She repeated time and again that everything she did was for Jesus and that she saw herself as "God's pencil," simply an instrument of the love of God. Cardinal Bernardin was for many a model of a church leader who led by example; and his book *The Gift of Peace* stands as one of the finest contemporary spiritual journals, a chronicle of his overcoming great stress and coming to deal with his slow dying of cancer. Francis, Teresa, and Catherine are all examples of people who, in their own times and places, sought to live the gospel by using their talents to give glory to God. In this book, though, I will pay special attention to the example of Ignatius of Loyola (1491–1556), who wrote an influential work called *The Spiritual Exercises* that grew out of his own struggles to grow closer to God. It is Ignatius's sixteenth-century text that is the inspiration for the title of this book. In fact, the very structure of this book is an adaptation of Ignatius's ideas, which many people have used in their spiritual lives. In particular, the order of brothers and priests that Ignatius founded, the Society of Jesus (Jesuits), uses the *Spiritual Exercises* in its spiritual formation, and on the campuses of many Jesuit high schools, colleges, and retreat centers around the country, this same text provides the basis for retreats that many ordinary Christians undertake.

If we are to understand spirituality, we can begin by taking a look at how Ignatius wrote about it in his text: spirituality is a practice, a regular endeavor through which we come to build our lives on the love of God—to order our lives according to God's plan for us. Its focus, then, is not primarily ourselves but, rather, God. In naming his spiritual practices "exercises," Ignatius sought to suggest something about how we ought to approach them: as undertakings we must repeat again and again in order to progress slowly toward a goal. We can see spiritual exercises, then, as a part of regular maintenance for the soul. If we practice them, we will give ourselves the chance to know God more intimately and to know God's will for us. Why is this important? Because, to paraphrase the theme of Psalm 139, God knows us better than we know ourselves. If God called us into existence and continues to intimately shape our existence every second, then God counts every hair on our heads and wants our good. Too often our lives bring us suffering, which seems so meaningless; and our natural reaction is to fight our suffering—and often God, too—in order to rid ourselves of it. Faith, I think, is the gift that enables us to suspend our judgments so that we might retain the belief that even through our suffering, God seeks our ultimate good.

The key word here is *ultimate.* Clearly, when I am suffering, I can't see any good in it. But if my concern is my ultimate good, then there are times when I must inevitably accept suffering. Back to our model, then: if my life were devoted to the elimination of all suffering, then I could never grow strong. I would avoid all exercise because exercise sometimes involves certain levels of pain (no pain, no gain, right?).

Taking this a step further, though, let us recognize that the objective is not pain per se—not all pain is acceptable. There is a difference between the pain of my burning lungs after a good hard cardiovascular workout and the pain of a pulled muscle. Athletes must learn to distinguish good pain from bad pain, and in so doing, they learn how to tolerate the good and avoid the bad. Similarly, then, in the spiritual life, we must be concerned with learning how God helps us confront certain kinds of suffering that help us grow and how he helps us avoid the suffering that only breaks us down. Moreover, we can see from this example that the spiritual life must be more than simply avoiding suffering; rather, it must be learning to discern among types of suffering and accepting the kind that leads us to greater spiritual growth.

One of the most memorable experiences I have of my early training is a morning spent doing set after set of leg exercises. By the end of the hour or so we all spent doing this, we were exhausted, and our leg muscles were on fire. Our coach instructed us to do one last exercise, a so-called wall sit, in which people stand holding their backs against a wall while keeping the legs bent at a ninety-degree angle. Try it—it's incredibly hard to do it for any significant length of time; we had to do it when we were already tired. I remember actually starting to cry because my legs hurt so much! After the ordeal was over, I was barely able to walk away, and the next day, I was almost unable to climb a set of stairs. What was important about that workout was that it forced me to confront my natural desire to avoid physical pain and my desire to become a stronger athlete. You may have heard the slogan "mind over matter"—it points to this idea of developing an attitude to confront pain for a greater good. It is an important idea for any serious athlete. I think about this same idea for the spiritual life because at a certain point, we must confront the need to pray when it seems difficult or meaningless. Not all spirituality is fun; not all of it bears immediate fruit. But the important idea is that we must develop a long-term understanding of spiritual goods. More precisely, we must remember that in steering us toward our ultimate good, God moves us through times of suffering to our ultimate happiness in God's presence.

A spiritual workout is first about confronting the reality of God and the reality of ourselves. This will involve some pain because the sad fact is that our lives often involve choices that lead us away from God—what in traditional language is called "sin." In fact, Jesus' own advice on how to live was to first "repent," or identify the wrong things we've done so we don't do them again. This advice makes sense; the only way we can get better at anything is by understanding the wrong ways of doing it. Coaches counsel their athletes on how to avoid mistakes; ministers counsel their flocks on how to avoid mistakes. The second thing a spiritual workout involves, then, is building good habits in place of the bad ones. If we want to develop our skills, we must not only learn what we're doing wrong; we must also learn how to do it right.

Doing spiritual workouts will help us to get rid of our bad habits, our sins, and to develop a stronger practice of living according to our ultimate good. They will help us to become better human beings by practicing the love of God and neighbor; and in so doing, we will live happier lives.

I'm racing toward the finish line to win the prize of God's ultimate calling in Jesus Christ. Every one of us who is spiritually mature has to think this way. (Phil 3:14–15 my translation)

WHAT ARE SPIRITUAL EXERCISES?

Ignatius (the Latin version of his name) the saint began life as Iñigo the tough guy. He was a hard-core kind of guy; he never did anything halfway. He was used to having it all: he was a nobleman from the Basque region of northern Spain, wealthy and good-looking, and ready for a life in the fast lane. He spent his early life in pursuit of glory, as a soldier under the Spanish crown. Everything in his life, up to a certain point, made him think of himself as being better than most people. He writes, describing himself, "Up to the age of twenty-six he was a man given to the vanities of the world; and what he enjoyed most was warlike sport, with a great and foolish desire to win fame."[1] But one tragic event forced him to completely rethink his self-image and his views of other people and God. This event marked the beginning of a terribly difficult process of change in his life. It was, for him, excruciatingly slow, painful, and seemingly without meaning for a long time. By the end, though, he was a changed man. One writer describes well the kind of process that Iñigo underwent, a process that all of us face: we live our lives forward but understand it backward. When Iñigo looked back, he saw the hand of God, even though he didn't realize it as he was living through it.

When he was twenty-six, Iñigo was in a fortress that the French were attacking. He describes how other officers were ready to surrender; but Iñigo—taking the hard-core attitude—persuaded them to fight. In the mayhem that followed, his leg was shattered by a cannonball, and he was captured by the French. They treated him kindly; eventually he was released and sent home. But by that point, his leg had healed so badly that it was misshapen and shorter than the other.

To the vain Iñigo, this was unbearable. He asked doctors if it could be healed, for with his ambitions, he could not stomach the idea of being disfigured. The doctors told him, though, that to heal the leg properly would be horribly painful; they would have to break it again, and he would face a long convalescence. Gritting his teeth, he told them to do it. He suffered awful pain, but he eventually began to recover.

It was during this slow, boring period of his life that he looked for something to do. He was confined to bed, which was (for him) bad enough; but even when he had to sit still, he was usually able to take some pleasure in reading stories about knights. Unfortunately for him at the time, the place where he was staying had none; the only books available were about religion. But he was so bored that he began reading. The stories of the saints particularly intrigued him, similar as they were to the stories about knights. The saints, though, were spiritual heroes, not military heroes, and he began to like learning their stories. Over time, he came to an important realization: reading about these "spiritual heroes" left him with a greater sense of peace than his earlier reading about knights and warfare. This experience left a lasting impression on him and was instrumental in his later work developing the Spiritual Exercises.

Over time, the contrast between his desires for fame and his desires for spiritual heroism became more pronounced. He wrote:

When he was thinking of those things of the world he took much delight in them, but afterwards, when he was tired and put them aside, he found himself dry and dissatisfied. But when he thought of going to Jerusalem barefoot, and of eating nothing but plain vegetables and of practicing all the other rigors that he saw in the saints, not only was he consoled when he had these thoughts, but even after putting them aside he remained satisfied and joyful.[2]

This experience, Iñigo later realized, was part of God's work in his life. He wrote, "Little by little he came to recognize the difference between the spirits that were stirring, one from the devil, the other from God."[3] Not long after this realization, he had a vision of Mary and Jesus, which moved him so strongly that he resolved from then on to completely relinquish everything he had sought in his desires for fame and wealth. He set his eyes only on growing in the knowledge and love of God. The mature Ignatius of Loyola could see that God was trying to speak to the young Iñigo. Learning how to hear God's voice was what Ignatius would eventually call "discernment," and this forms the heart of his Spiritual Exercises.

We can make a couple of observations based on Iñigo's experience. First: sometimes God works on us when we're depressed, or lonely, or grieving, or lost. Iñigo was in a bad way during his long convalescence; he was an adventure seeker (the sixteenth-century equivalent of an adrenaline addict) and so could not stand having to stay in bed for months on end. But it was due to this period of having to quiet down that he could listen for the voice of God, which whispered to him through his imagination. The second observation, then, is that we can discern the voice of God by paying attention to the things rattling around in our brains (but *only* if we pay attention!). Iñigo did not begin some spiritual search; he did not go out looking for God. But he did practice a little bit of self-knowledge: he recognized what it felt like when he thought about adventure, and he recognized what it felt like when he thought about sainthood.

We can take these observations as suggestions for a very basic spiritual exercise, imitating what Iñigo was forced into by circumstance. The exercise (call it a kind of spiritual warm-up) is simple:

1. Be quiet (turn off radios, TVs, computers, video games; close books, magazines, etc.).
2. Think about what really makes you happy.

For many people, step 1 is nearly impossible. We are so accustomed to having noise around that silence can make us uncomfortable. If you live in a busy area, silence is rare, so go to a church or a park or someplace where you can eliminate distractions. Once you do that, you'll probably notice how much "internal noise" we deal with: things you have to do today, things you forgot to do yesterday, things that happened to you on the way to work, whatever—they barge in on your attempts to be quiet. But keep trying! If it helps, focus your attention on just breathing. Another idea is to start with your toes and become aware of physical sensations, slowly moving up your feet into your legs and all the way up to your head. By focusing on these sensations, you start to turn your mental focus away from the world and in toward yourself. Eventually, you may feel ready to focus on step 2. What really makes you happy? Think about what you've done over the past day, the past week, the past month, the past year, the key moments of your life. What has produced lasting happiness? Move beyond the things that have been temporarily fun; focus instead on what has helped you to retain a feeling of joy toward just being alive. Think about the basic elements of your life that you take for granted: the way your body works; the way your mind works; the people close to you; the things you're proud of; the life events that have given you the most joy; the things you look forward to. What do these things tell you about yourself? How do they reveal to you the way God has made you? Repeat these practices several times in order to get used to the practice of focusing your attention.

Several things may happen. Some will feel a sense of gratefulness for what makes them happy. Others may feel disappointment, or loss, or even despair. If these negative feelings happen, don't dwell on them; simply acknowledge that they exist and recognize that they may be a sign that it is time to change your life. This, I think, is what happened to Ignatius. In recognizing that he had been making life choices based on a pretty shaky notion of happiness, he knew that he had to find something more permanent. This was the beginning of his conversion.

My friend once told me of the experience that led him to stop smoking. He was out playing with his four-year-old son, a whirlwind of energy. The little boy was so excited that his dad was out there with him, and he kept urging, "Catch me, Dad! Catch me, Dad!" as he ran around the yard. After a couple minutes of chasing little Jake around, my friend was exhausted. He had been smoking since his teens and so did not have very good lungs. He was unable to keep up with the four-year-old. In describing this experience a couple of years later, he spoke of how painful it was to realize that he simply could not do what was so valuable to him. But with the wisdom of hindsight, he was able to acknowledge gratefully that it was that experience that led him to the difficult decision of quitting smoking. Today he is healthier for it and much more able to chase his son around the yard.

The experience of confronting one's own bad choices is never easy. It is necessary, though, if we are ever to grow. And sometimes the way we confront our bad choices is, unfortunately, when they cause us pain. We are very stubborn creatures and will tend not to change things unless they hurt us. Pain, then, can sometimes be the necessary impetus for our spiritual growth. Just like we don't know we've caused our bodies injury unless we have some pain, we often don't know we've caused our souls injury unless we have some pain. And while this doesn't mean we should go looking for pain, we should let our pain tell us that it's time to change. The good news is that Jesus repeatedly promised that God heals us.

Iñigo confronted his spiritual pain and realized that it was pointing him toward a real life change. By the end of his recovery period, he was thinking about how he could take his energy, which had previously been about glorifying himself, and use it to glorify God. He writes about his desire to do stupendous acts for God, like a kind of spiritual hero. If he read of a certain saint's strict spiritual practices, Iñigo thought about how he could go one step further. In his autobiography, he writes of this period with a certain self-criticism, for he understood later in his life that this early period was a romanticized kind of spirituality. Many people fall into a similar pattern, thinking of spirituality in grand terms but missing it in the most basic, everyday ways. I've seen it among college students, who very often are willing to go and work in soup kitchens, travel to Appalachia or South America and do service work, or devote hours to participating in retreats, but don't apply this same kindness and generosity in their sexual lives, for example. One writer has described the spiritual life as involving first a movement of self-knowledge, then a movement away from self-centeredness. Many of us get stuck, though, in a very self-centered spirituality.

Over time, Iñigo made various attempts to render glory to God through his actions. Eventually, he settled himself into a rugged life in a cave outside Manresa, in northern Spain, and put together his observations about the spiritual life that would become the *Spiritual Exercises*. In the *Spiritual Exercises,* we see someone with a keen sense of psychology, even before there was a science of the mind. Iñigo was fully aware of how difficult the spiritual life can be, since he himself had led the kind of life that was based on the kind of choices we all make today: choices based on what's fashionable, what other people are doing, what's new and exciting. Reflecting on his earlier life, he came to conclusions that challenge our ways of thinking: "I don't care if I have health or sickness, riches or poverty, honor or dishonor, a long life or a short one. I care only about the things that lead me to my ultimate good, which is God's love." [4]

In short, Iñigo formulated his Spiritual Exercises as a way that people could get rid of their illusions and focus on what is most important in life. He used the Spiritual Exercises among his friends when he went back to college, and during these years, a group of young men banded together under the name "The Company of Jesus," or the "Jesuits" (as they were sarcastically called—like we might say "Jesus-ites"). This small group accepted the name, unafraid as they were of being labeled as Jesus freaks. They didn't care what other people thought; they were rebels and proud of it. And what gave them such a strong focus on their spiritual lives was the constant practice of Iñigo's Exercises.

There is a certain goodness and integrity to such single-mindedness as we see in Iñigo and his early companions. Today we recognize a similar attitude in those who prepare for the Olympics. During the coverage of the recent Olympiads, the networks would sometimes run stories about certain athletes: how they overcame obstacles, how they faced personal tragedies, how they maintained devotion to their athletic pursuits. It is easy to cheer on someone who has faced a long struggle to compete; we laud their courage and perseverance. I think we all recognize on a basic level that there is something noble about this kind of long-term vision toward a goal. And I want to suggest that if we carry this same kind of attitude into our thinking about God and about spirituality, we will be better off than those who just want a quick "spiritual fix." If spirituality is about discerning God's will for our lives, then it must be a lifelong pursuit.

HOW CAN SPIRITUAL EXERCISES HELP POSTMODERN PEOPLE?

It is difficult to read any sixteenth-century text, let alone to see it as a model for postmodern living. What makes the *Spiritual Exercises* remarkable is Ignatius's keen psychological insights. He did not see himself inventing some new kind of spiritual practice as much as having people pay attention to very basic forms of prayer: reading the Bible, meditating, asking God for help. Ignatius's Exercises are all about paying attention in prayer. They are not about reciting the right words, or undertaking some amazing spiritual devotion, or even traveling to the ends of the world doing acts of charity. More important, they don't rely on outdated understandings of God, or Jesus, or faith, or piety—they leave a great deal up to each person, to figure out who God is, who Jesus is, what faith is, and what piety is. But they do this recognizing that we all begin with limited ideas of these things, and so they emphasize that we need proper coaching (more on this in chapter 1). Ignatius's Spiritual Exercises are great for postmodern people because they invite us to learn spirituality by doing it.

This is important. There are two significant changes in the way people practice spirituality today, in contrast to Ignatius's time or even our grandparents' time. First, we live in a much more pluralistic world. The world has shrunk; we have the Internet and cell phones and up-to-the-minute, live news reports all around the world. Many will remember the broadcasts of the millennium celebrations all around the world on New Year's Eve 2000, when they could turn on the TV and instantly see people in Tokyo, Sydney, Moscow, Cairo, Paris, London, New York, Chicago, Los Angeles, and Honolulu celebrating the coming of their respective midnights. It was, and is, very easy to learn about people very different from ourselves, and so it is difficult to maintain strong feelings about the rightness of one way of thinking and the wrongness of another. Cities and towns all around the world have become more diverse ethnically and religiously; and as a result, people are forced to confront their differences in order to build better communities.

Second, we don't treat authority the way people used to. People have learned to trust the judgments of their own consciences more than the judgments of religious or political authorities. This is a result, I think, of having immediate access to the world's knowledge at the click of a mouse. We simply can know more than our predecessors. Of course, the major difficulty is that there is too much information; we have to learn how to sift through it all. But even here we trust ourselves. We don't want others telling us what to learn and not to learn.

What makes us postmodern people is that we live in a new era and approach the world in ways different from the ways our parents or grandparents did. Philosophers describe the "modern" era as lasting from around the sixteenth century (the time of Ignatius) until the twentieth, a four-hundred-year stretch that involved the expansion of scientific knowledge, the exploration of new lands (and eventually outer space), and an optimism about the future of civilization. In our recent history, we can see evidence of this modern approach to the world in the ways that older generations thought about themselves. Even after the Second World War, which signaled for many the beginning of the end of the modern era, many people returned home, got jobs, raised families, paid taxes, voted, went to church, saved money, and did well. For this generation, duty and responsibility were key ideas; and this means that they had a certain level of trust of authority. Their children, the baby boomers, reacted against authority. When they came of age in the 1960s, they changed the way people looked at authority. Even the most basic glance at the major events of that decade in the United States and worldwide shows how things were changing: the Cold War; the assassinations of the Kennedys, Martin Luther King Jr., and Malcolm X; the Second Vatican Council of the Catholic Church; the rise of pop music and the phenomenon of Woodstock; the Vietnam War; and eventually Watergate. Many factors contributed to a growing suspicion toward authority and led many to greater and greater pessimism about the modern ideal of progress.

Our postmodern age is about the crisis of authority. Our grandparents respected it; our parents reacted against it; today we don't give it that much thought. With these cultural differences come differences in spirituality. For if spirituality is about the way we as human beings respond to the invitation of God, then the only way we can "do" spirituality is through our concrete, culturally and historically situated lives. In our culture and in our history, authority is a problem; and so our spirituality manifests a certain ambivalence toward what has been passed on to us from religious authorities. Our grandparents, in large part, practiced a spirituality that was about obeying the Ten Commandments, the words of Jesus, and the local minister or priest. Many in our parents' generation (though not all) began reacting against these traditional notions of authority and began their own spiritual searches, which for some involved moving outside the traditional sources of Christian spirituality toward, for example, Eastern religious practices. Popular figures such as the Beatles captured attention and inspired followers to see religion not as something we are bound to by birth but, rather, as something we can choose by opening our minds beyond what we have been taught.

The consequence for the postmodern generation has been an authority vacuum. Many have been brought up with little or no religion whatsoever, sometimes because of the deliberate choice of parents not to force any religion on their children. Our interest in spirituality has arisen because we still face the same basic questions that all people face: questions about God, love, death, suffering, meaning, and so on. But we face these questions, in many cases, with no religious vocabulary, no way to talk about these questions because we lack the language and the symbolic world within which we can make sense of them. Many in the postmodern generation describe themselves as spiritual but not religious—interested in developing a spirituality but not so interested in having to go through what seem to be the "motions" that are inherent in religion.

What makes the *Spiritual Exercises* a helpful guide for us postmoderns is its insistence that we can come to know God by coming to know ourselves better. Ignatius was a bit of a maverick in his early life, as I described; the spiritual practices he worked through were not simply repeating old formulas but, rather, a fresh attempt to make sense of God's will. For us, these same exercises offer a chance to explore on our own terms, with our own thoughts, the same question. The exercises are not about determining who is the best Christian, or who knows the Bible the best, or who is most obedient to the laws of the church, or anything along those lines. They are about seeking to understand the movements of God in our own lives, our own experiences, by paying attention to our imagination. They are built on a basic trust that God will self-reveal to us and that we can recognize God even if we don't have doctorates in theology or even if we aren't particularly religious. In fact, this book can be useful both for people who are religious and for people who may have very little positive experience with religion but who still want to confront the tough questions in their lives.

The bottom line is that postmodern people need God no less than people of earlier times, even though we live in an age that makes it hard to know how to find God. There are so many places that our hunger for God manifests itself; the tragedy is that too often we aren't even aware of this hunger. Ignatius's Spiritual Exercises can help us to first recognize our hunger for God—which can be painful—and further, they can help us to respond to the God who is already present to us, inviting us into a deeper relationship.

This book has two parts. Part 1 introduces the idea of spiritual workouts by looking at some basic notions of what constitutes authentic prayer. Chapter 1 is devoted to an overview of some basic ideas on how to pray. Chapter 2 offers two specific exercises, which will be especially helpful for those who are beginners at prayer. Chapter 3 then addresses how to get the most out of workouts, focusing on seven regular practices during the time of prayer. What will come out in these first three chapters is that Ignatius offers flexibility in prayer, recognizing that different people will pray differently. These exercises are about coming to better understand ourselves as conversation partners with God. I suggest that you read the first three chapters, then take some time to go back over the exercises in chapters 2 and 3. Spend some time practicing them before moving on to chapter 4.

Chapter 4 is the central chapter, both in terms of its being in the center of the book and in terms of its being the heart of the spiritual workout. In that chapter, we shall take a look at what Ignatius identifies as the most fundamental attitude that we must have in order to grow spiritually. The first three chapters lead to this chapter, and the following four build upon it. The principles discussed in chapter 4 are the bedrock upon which a mature spirituality can be constructed, but for many, the foundation itself may need some work. As you practice the exercises in chapters 2 and 3, pay attention to what you learn about your own spirituality so that by the time you reach chapter 4, you have a stronger sense of your own foundation. You may need to spend some time simply working on developing a stronger foundation: a stronger faith that God is intimately helping you construct your daily life.

Part 2 is a guide to more advanced prayer, based on the core of the Spiritual Exercises. The chapters in part 2 represent four weeks of prayer (originally designed for a thirty-day retreat), each week focusing on a different element of the mystery of Christian faith. These chapters are best read in order, though it is possible to use any of the chapters as a single spiritual workout on different occasions. The structure of the four weeks is pretty simple. First, we confront our bad choices; second, we ask which direction we want our lives to lead; third, we consider the example of Jesus; and fourth, we focus on the promises of God to care for our ultimate good. There is, then, a movement in the four workouts, from our narrow vision of how to live and toward a reliance on God's will for our lives. Again, the objective of these workouts is to build our lives on a vision of our ultimate good, which God knows better than we can. It is best to take your time with the suggestions in these chapters. Don't think about each workout being a single day's prayer but, rather, remember that each of these workouts was originally designed to last a week of retreat (meaning that a person did nothing all day but pray, eat, and sleep!). So take your time moving through these workouts—pay attention to yourself and your needs. As I explain in chapter 1, it is important at some point in your spiritual workouts to rely on the guidance of a director, and so I encourage you to use the resources listed at the end of this book to locate one.

Whether you are a novice at prayer or have always tried to live a Christian life, you can gain something in these spiritual workouts. It is worth mentioning, especially if you are unfamiliar with prayer, that like anything else, learning to pray takes time. No one is going to become an Olympic gold medalist right away; no one is going to turn into a mystic right away. In both cases, we need to develop a long-range vision. For Ignatius, that vision was simple: he wanted to know the will of God to achieve his ultimate happiness. I invite you to practice these workouts, to discern God's will for your life, too.

1

What Is a
Spiritual
Workout?

what to expect in spiritual workouts

I FIND IT INTERESTING TO BE AT A WEDDING OR SOME OTHER PUBLIC ceremony when a minister or priest utters the words, "Let us pray." Almost always, the room becomes quiet, heads bow, hands are folded, postures are straightened. It's as if God won't listen unless we behave like second-grade students on their best behavior when the teacher enters the room. What's sometimes even funnier to me is that after this solemn exercise, sometimes people will resume telling off-color jokes, gossiping about so-and-so, or whatever. The implication: we have to be on our best behavior when God is around, but after we've dismissed God, we can get back to the fun!

I mention this observation to highlight that if we are going to pray in a way that isn't deceiving to ourselves, then we have to have some basic ideas straight. We must, in other words, have some legitimate ideas about what we're trying to do. Imagine a child learning that she is about to join a soccer league and wanting to make a good impression on the other kids. She tells her mom, "I'm going to practice soccer today so I can be as good as my friends." Mom smiles and pats her daughter on the back and watches as the little girl goes out the door to practice. After an hour, the girl comes back into the house and announces proudly, "I'm going to be great, Mom! I can catch the soccer ball every time!" Mom realizes, with some chagrin, that the little girl has been using her hands for the last hour to throw and catch a football, not a soccer ball.

Sometimes I think people's efforts at prayer are a little like this. They spend a great deal of effort at *something*, but that something may have very little to do with God. Their efforts come from misunderstandings, or partial understandings, or bad teaching, or whatever; and when they complain that they don't feel like anything is happening, they blame God and give up. This chapter will address the basic question of what prayer is like and what to expect when undertaking spiritual workouts. It will focus on five areas that Ignatius identified as important throughout his work: fundamentals, coaching, dedication, discernment, and the practice of finding God in all things.

FUNDAMENTALS

Openness

The single most common mistake people make in their spiritual lives is wanting God to follow their lead. Especially in a world in which we have so many demands, we feel an intense need to keep everything organized so as not to feel overwhelmed. Unfortunately, for many people, God fits into a neat little box that is opened only once in a while, whether it be on Sunday mornings or when reading or out enjoying nature. If we want to take God seriously, though, *we* must be the ones ready to follow *God's* lead. Gerard W. Hughes has it right when he writes about a "God of surprises," a person whose presence in our lives often calls us beyond the narrow limits of our expectations.[1] We might, however, take comfort in the words of someone like Peter when Jesus first met him: "Leave me, Lord. I'm a sinner." Initial reticence to pay attention to God's invitation is not uncommon, for his call pulls us outside of the comfort zones we create for ourselves in a scary world. If we think about it, responding to God's invitation should be something we want to do—as scary as it is, it is about trusting that God wants our ultimate good and believing that God is more capable than we are of leading us to it. According to the Gospels, God is intimately concerned about our well-being: God counts the hairs on our heads; seeks for us like a shepherd when we are lost; issues invitations to us to join in a feast; waits like a father for a lost son; holds us close like a mother with her baby. As a father, I find these parenting images especially meaningful, for they describe for me a God whose feelings for me are as profound as those I feel for my children.

Our posture toward God is often skewed because we work hard to create a life for ourselves in the midst of economic or social conditions that are not always helpful. To cite one example, my wife once shared with me that as a child, she was terrified of the idea of having to commit to a religious vocation—becoming a nun—because all the stories she had heard as a child about faith involved priests or nuns. As much as I respect those who have religious vocations (including a family member, friends, and coworkers), I realize that this is only one of the many ways God calls people to live lives that reflect faith. As my wife grew older, she realized that religious life was not her vocation; she instead began to look at the specific characteristics and talents with which she could express her faith.

Some people seem to have the image that in order to follow God, they have to do something radically different than what they enjoy or do well. They are afraid to let God into the mainstream of their lives; they prefer to keep God on the periphery so as not to upset the careful balance. They wish to hold on to what they think is valuable about their lives, afraid of letting go of the things in their lives that help them to feel important: job, money, education, connections, whatever.

Addressing this situation, a priest friend of mine from Papua New Guinea once gave a sermon in which he told a parable of a man who loved living in his tropical paradise. Having been born on the island where his parents, grandparents, and great-grandparents had always lived, he held in his heart a special place for the beauty of the palm trees, the white sand, the sloping mountains, the gentle climate. This man, approaching death, told his loved ones to place some island sand into each of his hands when he died, so that he might hold on to the memory of his beloved place forever. They did, and so the man proceeded to the gates of heaven still clutching the sand. At the gate, he was warmly greeted and told that as soon as he emptied his hands of the sand, he could enter into eternal joy. The man was crushed, for he could not let go of what he loved so much, and so he waited. He waited, the parable goes, for a long, long time; so long that at last his hands grew weary and could no longer hold the sand. It eventually slipped through his fingers, lost forever. At that moment, Jesus came to him, holding the man as he sobbed at the loss of his memory, and said, "Come now, and enter into your rest." With that, Jesus walked with the man through the gates of heaven, where before them both stretched out the entirety of the man's beloved island.

The parable challenges us to consider what we hold on to that prevents us from turning our lives over to God, and whether it is indeed wise to try to seek our happiness apart from what God would help us to find. The fundamental posture of authentic prayer, Ignatius counsels, is that of openness to the will of God for our lives, for it is through that will that we will be led to our very reason for existing in the first place. In short, God knows our hearts better even than we do, and so when we pray, we ought to seek greater understanding of God's will. To put it differently, our prayer must involve more than just asking for things that we'd like. While it is good to ask God for good things, as Jesus himself taught us to do ("Ask, and it will be given you; seek, and you will find" [Mt 7:7]), this is not the only way to pray. If we take seriously the idea that God is inviting us into a relationship based on love, then our prayer will naturally involve things like appreciation (saying thanks) and praise but also, at times, resentment and anger. We fool ourselves if we think any relationship is always sweet and pleasant. What Jesus counseled was persistence in prayer, even during the times when it seems God is not listening.

There is a story Ignatius recounts in his autobiography that illustrates a kind of openness. It seems that after Ignatius recovered from his leg injury, he was having difficulty deciding what to do with his life. He resolved to travel to Jerusalem on a pilgrimage and began making plans. On the road to a place where he was to collect some money, he encountered someone who, in Ignatius's mind, defamed the Virgin Mary. Ignatius stewed over this encounter for some time, finding it hard to decide what to do about it. Ultimately, finding himself torn between chasing after the man and killing him, or continuing on his way in preparation for his pilgrimage (and after that, a life of penance), he resolved to let the mule he was riding on make the decision. Up ahead was a fork in the road: one direction took him toward where the man was staying, one in the other direction Ignatius was traveling. When the mule came to the fork in the road, he resolved, Ignatius would wait for the mule to decide which road to take. The mule took the road that did not lead to where the man was staying, and so Ignatius did not kill the man.

This story was for Ignatius a metaphor for the spiritual life. By that point in his life, he could recognize that the desire to kill his traveling companion was not motivated by love of God, and yet the desire was still there. It was a remnant of what Ignatius later called a "disordered affection," a skewed way of feeling about things in the world. Having grown up with the image of the knight as the supreme manifestation of manly virtue, Ignatius developed an emotional and psychological predisposition toward thinking of all things according to the standards of chivalry. Through his conversion experience, though, he recognized these standards as being different from God's. Allowing the mule to make this formative decision in his life was tantamount to recognizing his own inadequacy to determine right from wrong.

An important prerequisite for doing spiritual workouts is openness: the sensibility that ultimately God is in charge and that whatever desires, ideas, fears, hopes, or expectations we bring into prayer might be transformed. It is bringing an open mind and heart into prayer, anticipating only that it will give me the freedom to change according to the ways that God wants me to change—not against my will but because of it. Like Ignatius, we may come to recognize that the things we think we want in life are, ultimately, of little value. We may come to a point when we can look back at our earlier life plans and laugh at our own ideas! This is clearly what happened to Ignatius as he was writing his autobiography. His mature outlook on life was very different from that of his youth.

In introducing his Spiritual Exercises, Ignatius writes about them as follows:

> The name "spiritual exercises" is given to any way we prepare or make ready our souls to get rid of our skewed feelings, and then once they are gone, to seek out and find God's will for our lives and our ultimate good.[2]

A regime of spiritual workouts is about giving ourselves the opportunity to form our lives based on what God wants for us, even if that may be different from what we have planned. For some, this idea may sound difficult; we don't like the idea of giving up what we've done with our lives and running off to join a religious order. But what I'm trying to suggest is that whatever God wills for us will be the fulfillment of our deepest desires as human beings. True, some have been called and are called to change their lifestyles, like Ignatius did (or St. Paul before him), but many will simply be called to do what they are doing with renewed depth. We can take some comfort from the stories of saints who have been called into life-changing conversions, for again and again, what characterizes the life of trust in God is joy. God calls us into making our lives what they should be, clearing away the things that may have taken us off track. What Ignatius calls "skewed feelings" or "disordered affections" are really those things we *think* we like, based on our circumstances. A spiritual workout helps us to see them in a greater perspective; it helps us to let go of the things we *think* we like so that we might be more free to attach ourselves to what gives us more permanent joy.

Honesty

A second common problem people have with prayer is that they form elaborate ideas about what it's supposed to look like; and no matter what the circumstances are, they hold on to these ideas. Underlying the whole of Ignatius's writing is a sense of sobriety about the spiritual life, its demand for honesty on the part of the person doing the workouts. We cannot pretend that prayer is always going to put us in a peaceful mood or that we will leave it with a profound sense of having been touched by God. Sometimes prayer leaves us dry and weary; sometimes it makes us angry; other times it makes us feel terribly alone. It is important to acknowledge these feelings, while not concluding that they mean God doesn't love us. Early on especially, people for whom formal prayer is new may feel like nothing is happening. It is important not to pretend in our prayer, for only by acknowledging what we feel can we make any sort of progress.

When I coached collegiate rowing, I came across many great people who were also very dedicated athletes. They wanted to prove themselves able to perform the workouts I assigned and show that they could handle the stresses on their bodies. They saw workouts as challenges to be overcome and wanted to prove to themselves that they could do whatever was necessary to make fast boats. I found that novice rowers especially were unlikely to tell me about any problems they were having, because they didn't want to appear weak or incompetent to me or to their friends on the team. So, often, they would simply ignore problems. After a time, I learned to look for telltale signs: fatigue, stress, lowering interest levels; and so I learned to ask questions about their experiences in training. In many cases, the difficulties were due to simple technical errors (like the placement of the hands on the oar) that, if addressed directly, could lead to more-efficient performance. Often, I had to coax out their problems: "What do you feel? Where does it hurt?" If they told me what was going on, most times I could help them address the problem.

A similar dynamic takes place in our spiritual lives. If we assume everything is supposed to go smoothly all the time, frustration can set in the first time we feel different from the way we expect to feel. Being honest in our workouts means, first, acknowledging when we are finding them difficult or pointless. Often, this is simply a reflection of how our expectations are not matching the reality of the situation. Coupled with a sense of openness, honesty can allow us to recognize problems but deal with them in a more fluid way.

I'd like to share an analogy from rowing that I find helpful here. A key to rowing well is to have a certain flexibility about what is going on. On any given day, the water could be choppy, the wind could be strong, the current could be fast—all of these things affect how a person or crew feels in a boat. Novice rowers often make the mistake of trying too hard under these different circumstances to keep the boat in perfect balance: they hold the oar handles with white knuckles, muscling through the strokes in an attempt to keep moving smoothly. What invariably happens, though, is that the boat (which is narrow and thus hard to balance) tips from side to side, even for crews who are experienced. If someone is gripping the oar handle too tightly, it can tip the boat even more wildly; the oar acts like a pole striking the water, pushing the boat down to the other side. Good coaches know to counsel their crews to stay relaxed, to allow the boat to tip slightly from side to side, but to focus on what is more important: keeping it moving fast. Instead of gripping the oars tightly, people should stay relaxed and absorb whatever tips should happen.

What I find illustrative about this metaphor is that it suggests something about expectations and effort. When our expectations are wrong, our effort sometimes has to increase; we can grow tired more quickly and sense that things are not going well. On the other hand, if our expectations are legitimate, we will often find that problems that arise do not bother us as much; we simply adapt to whatever

comes our way. In prayer, this attitude can be helpful. Instead of trying with every ounce of energy to do prayer the way we think we
should (good posture, pleasant words, a saintly smile on our faces), we
can instead try to be realistic. We should expect that sometimes
"waves" will come our way—life situations that make it hard to
pray—but we can still keep our focus on a more long-term understanding of the spiritual life. It is important to allow ourselves to
change our workouts, based on the varying circumstances of our lives.

In my own life, this point was hard to learn. I had developed the
practice of formal prayer during college, having learned from the
Jesuits at the institutions where I studied. After a time, it felt like I
had achieved a certain rhythm, and I felt confident that the methods I
had learned would sustain me throughout my life. Yes, there were life
changes; moves, changes of jobs, marriage, and just growing up had
effects on my prayer life. But I was able to adapt and more or less
maintain a prayer life in spite of those changes.

But then came children! Life circumstances became very different,
and I found myself having real difficulty with prayer. My wife and I
encountered a long process of struggle that finally led to the adoption
of our first daughter. As I look back over the last couple of years, I
realize how much of my problems in prayer came as a result of not
dealing honestly with these struggles. I had developed a certain expectation about my spiritual life over my college and single years, and
this expectation may have hindered me somewhat when my life
changed. I could not pray the way I used to; I probably will never
again pray the way I used to. This is not to say what I did then was
wrong; rather, it is to recognize that I am now a different person.
Fortunately for me, a caring spiritual director helped me to understand this (I'll discuss spiritual direction more in the next section). It
took a long time to honestly confront what was going on; my own
unwillingness to confront God under difficult circumstances hindered
my ability to pray at all.

The spiritual life involves highs and lows, periods of what Ignatius
called "consolation" (comfort) and "desolation" (despair). We cannot
pretend that prayer is always going to make us happy at the moment

any more than we can pretend that life experiences will. Our spiritual lives, to state the obvious, are *our lives*—with all the attendant joy and grief that come with them. In order to construct our lives well, we must not fool ourselves with false images. The biblical term that is relevant here is *idolatry*, idol worship: the practice of making God into something more manageable. It is very easy to fall into idolatry because we all want to have control of the circumstances of our lives and to make God fit into the place we have assigned. Sometimes we need someone to tell us when we are doing this, because we can tend to be blind to the ways we do it ourselves. For this reason, Ignatius suggests that we need guides.

COACHING

Any serious athlete knows that training alone is often a bad idea. Since we can't actually watch ourselves perform, the only feedback we can have as individuals is through reflecting on what we are doing at the moment or thinking about it afterward. This practice of self-reflection is very important, to be sure; but it is inadequate. We need someone with an outside perspective who can tell us what we're doing well and what we're doing wrong, who can suggest ideas about how to get better.

This is especially true for novices. The first time a person tries a new sport, she is awkward and unused to the new physical demands, whether they include shooting a basket, running fast, or hitting a ball. A good coach will take a person's interest and provide encouragement and hints for how to improve, recognizing that the person's ego is still a bit fragile. Recently I participated in a "learn to row" day at our boathouse, when dozens of people showed up for the first time to have a try at what they considered a new and interesting activity. I'm always interested in helping out at events like these because I find it refreshing to meet people who want to try something new and are willing to feel a little silly as they get started. I've been involved in rowing, both as an athlete and as a coach, for over a dozen years; so it's nice to meet people who look at it with fresh eyes. I find that I, too, can learn something from them about what motivates them to try in the first place.

I was on the other side of this experience recently. I was at the beach and decided to try surfing. I met a man in his fifties who was the surf coach—he had been doing it for many years, and his attitude was contagious. In a short while, he was able not only to teach me the mechanics of riding waves but also to convey a real enthusiasm and love for the sport. On that first day, I walked away feeling as though I had learned something and looked forward to being able to try it again.

Prayer, like anything, takes time to learn. Good coaches help us to channel our enthusiasm in ways that make us look forward to doing it well. They can help us to avoid frustration by making sure we get off to the right start. Christian spirituality has recognized the value of tradition as an authoritative guide, a kind of coach for the spiritual life. Ignatius himself, though he was an innovator in some respects, did not really invent any new forms of prayer. On the contrary, he used what he considered to be useful guides for his own prayer life and adapted them to fit the needs of his situation. Today we are wise to follow his example by appealing to sources of spirituality that have some grounding in long-standing practice.

One obvious example is participation in a worshiping community. Sadly, many today who are interested in spirituality don't follow through with this step, which is necessary if we are to avoid deceiving ourselves. Spirituality cannot be a solitary endeavor; it must be grounded in the life of a community, or else it becomes little more than an isolated and ineffective version of self-help. Spirituality that is grounded in community is like the house built on rock that Jesus described (Mt 7:24); it is less likely to be blown away by the winds of change that inevitably move through our lives. When our spirituality arises from our participation in community, several things happen. First, we are challenged to see our prayer as one part of the larger exercise of living the Christian life, for we must apply our prayer to the ordinary problems of living with other people. This prevents us from treating spirituality solely as a private exercise. We will be in a position to encourage others in tough times; in turn, they can help us to perse-vere in periods of spiritual dryness. Second, participation in commu-nity worship means we will be confronting ideas that make us uncomfortable, pushing us outside of the natural comfort zones we develop in our spiritual lives. This point, I think, is difficult but important. It's easy to fall into patterns that must change as we grow. Third, we will begin to see our own spiritual lives in some perspective, by seeing the struggles and issues of people who are both younger and older than us. Seeing what younger people confront can make us cog-nizant of how we have grown; seeing what older people confront can make us cognizant of how much more we must still grow. Considering the spiritual journeys of people around us can help us to navigate the changes we, too, encounter. My hope is that as people come to see church as a place where people help each other grow in their spiritual lives, it might be transformed.

Ignatius understood that all Christians are called to practice the spiritual life in community but some are called further to deepen their relationship with God through more concerted efforts. As far back as the earliest centuries of Christian life, there are examples of men and women who elected to turn their backs on the society of their youth and devote themselves wholeheartedly to God. Some went literally empty-handed into the desert, where they practiced a kind of spiritual athleticism: subduing their minds and bodies through the constant practice of prayer. Over the centuries, we encounter stories of people whose spiritual practices sound astonishing, even absurd; the common bond is that these people sought a deeper knowledge of God by relin-quishing all things that might distract them. As noted earlier, Ignatius himself was enthralled by stories of spiritual athleticism, for it attracted the part of him that wanted to be better than anyone else. Later, it seems, he came to realize that there was a somewhat selfish motive in this attraction; but the core idea of devoting himself wholly to God was what impelled him in his vocation. He wisely recognized, though, that in order to pursue it, he needed the help of those who had themselves already been practicing their spirituality for some time.

An important part of his *Spiritual Exercises,* therefore, focuses on the role of the spiritual director, the person who acts as a kind of coach to the person seeking to understand the will of God. Today there are people all over the world who are trained in this capacity; many are involved in retreat centers and can help even people who have never prayed formally. (At the end of this book, there is a list of such retreat centers, which interested people can contact for further information on finding spiritual direction.)

The role of the spiritual director is to help a person see through his or her biases in order to more clearly know the will of God. He or she does not lecture or teach but, rather, helps the person see more clearly the movements of God in prayer. Teresa of Ávila, a mystic who lived at about the same time as Ignatius, wrote that in a good spiritual director, knowledge is more important than piety. In other words, a director is someone who has studied prayer and who (like many athletic coaches) is sometimes better at teaching others to do it than doing it personally. The bottom line is that spiritual direction is a skill different from prayer itself, for it involves understanding something about the way God communicates to people in prayer and the way people are likely to respond.

In this book I do not presuppose that you have immediate access to spiritual direction, but I encourage anyone who is interested in furthering his or her prayer life to consider it. What I do suggest, however, is that you not treat spirituality as something you can learn completely on your own. No one can run a marathon without someone to train her; no one can dig deeply into prayer without a spiritual director. In the earliest days of the church, we see that certain people were called to be spiritual leaders, people who had internalized the words and actions of Jesus and could communicate them to other people. From these times onward, it became clear that seeking God involved more than just good intentions—it also involved learning from those who had themselves already advanced on "the Way," as Christianity was first called in apostolic times. Today those who devote themselves to professional ministry are the inheritors of that tradition, and in my experience, they like nothing better than helping out someone who is truly interested in knowing the will of God.

DEDICATION

One of the unpleasant tasks I had to perform as a coach was to keep my athletes motivated to do the work they needed in order to compete at a high level. Often this took the form of cajoling or even threatening them to finish a workout—not in a sadistic way, of course, but with the understanding that when people get tired, they can sometimes get sloppy. Under these circumstances, it was very important for me to understand what workouts feel like: weariness, lack of motivation, and other factors can inhibit people from doing what they know they are capable of doing.

The hardest time to motivate athletes to do their work is after a difficult loss. At low points, people naturally start to ask questions about whether all the hard work pays off; and sometimes it's hard to come up with an answer. At such moments, the trust that teams have built over the course of the season becomes crucial, for without it the project would collapse.

Like anything else in life, prayer will involve highs and lows. We all know that it's easy to continue doing something when it makes us happy; but the opposite is true when it makes us depressed. But, as I suggested earlier, expectations are important: if a team absolutely refuses to believe that they can ever lose, then the first time they do lose will be particularly difficult. Realistically, it's important to understand (even with a hard-line, motivating "no lose" attitude) that there are going to be setbacks in any endeavor worth devoting energy to, so that when these setbacks occur, they can be seen as part of the larger picture. In the case of prayer, the larger picture involves consolation and desolation: periods when God's love and care seem obvious, and periods when God seems totally absent and unconcerned. In the times of desolation, Ignatius's counsel is clear: don't change anything. Stick to whatever resolutions you made during the period of consolation.

And during consolation, moreover, we should think about how our resolutions will affect us during the next period of desolation.

As a college athlete, I was impressed by the counsel one coach gave me about doing workouts: he said that as long as you do each one with as much intensity as you can, then on race day, you will have no regrets about your preparation. So I became accustomed to working as hard as I could every day, sometimes doing double workouts just so I could be sure I was giving everything I had. On certain days, especially in the middle of a dismal winter, I would have vastly preferred doing any number of other things: hanging out with friends, seeing a movie, going out, whatever. But every night, even on Fridays when everyone else seemed to be doing something interesting, I would head off to bed early so I could make the 5 A.M. wake-up and get to my workouts. There were times when I thought I was crazy to make such sacrifices, especially when we had some pretty disappointing results during race season. But I am still moved by the feeling of having no regrets, even in a losing cause—there's something about knowing that you tried as hard as possible to be your best.

Confronting the reality of highs and lows in any endeavor is hard, but unless we do it, chances are we will not succeed. How many people do you know who have made New Year's resolutions that lasted only a short time? Usually, people have great intentions that eventually fade because other life concerns choke them off. Confronting the reality of desolation in our prayer lives can help us take a realistic, farsighted view of what to expect: sometimes prayer will be boring or difficult or painful. But it is still worth doing. I am convinced that the twentieth-century monk and spiritual guide Thomas Merton was right when he wrote in a well-known prayer that our desire to know God is important to God, even when we don't particularly understand what is going on. Dedication in our prayer lives means simply that we expect periods of consolation and desolation, and that we do not place unrealistic demands on what prayer is supposed to feel like. Yes, sometimes it makes us feel good; it can bring us to periods of intense contemplation; it can help us to know God's loving care; it can confront us with the sheer beauty of creation. And it is wonderful when those things happen! But they are not the *reason* for prayer. Deepening our relationship with God is the reason, and so, as in any other relationship, we must be prepared to experience low points. Abandoning anything when it becomes difficult may prevent us from growing as human beings; abandoning prayer when it seems worthless may prevent us from knowing how God is changing us during these periods. Again, good coaching helps us to gain perspective on the low points in our spiritual lives, to understand that sometimes the greatest spiritual growth occurs at those times when we feel distant from God.

As I look back over my prayer life of the last decade or so, it is clear to me that times of desolation are necessary, not unlike periods of sleep in our daily lives or periods when fields lie fallow. In these examples, it seems to us like nothing is happening; but these periods make possible the growth that we can later see and understand. If we allow ourselves to prepare for the fact that sometimes desolation happens, we can give ourselves the chance to trust that God is preparing us for a more mature relationship when we are ready. It may be helpful to consider the example of Jesus on the cross: his moment of utter desolation led him to cry out to God, "Why have you abandoned me?" But as we know, that was not the last chapter in his story.

DISCERNMENT

Ignatius counseled that the key to the spiritual life, listening to God's will, is *discernment*. Discernment is a process in which we look at the different experiences we encounter in prayer and distinguish what is leading us toward God from what is leading us away from God.

Earlier I described how athletes must learn to distinguish good pain from bad pain. This may be a helpful starting point to think about discernment; we learn the practice through continued effort over time by asking questions about the effects of different experiences. An important theme in discernment is that it must involve more than just an immediate reaction to our prayer. As noted above, sometimes we will encounter painful times. Discernment helps us to understand how on occasion we must confront pain in order to grow, but it also helps us to recognize the times when the pain is too much for us and we must seek help.

In our time, sciences like psychology, sociology, neurobiology, and others have made us much more conscious of the different factors that affect our attitude toward life. Even on an intuitive level, though, most people understand how things like the weather, job stress, relationships, health, and other factors can make an impact on our spiritual lives. There are some days when everything seems to go wrong; it's hard for me not to get mad at God under such circumstances. While Ignatius was not trained in the modern sciences, he did nevertheless have what we would call today a keen psychological insight. He did understand how spirituality is tied up with these other factors, and so his rules for discernment are about trying to get a sense of what one is facing in prayer. To use an obvious example, imagine that you've got the flu, you've just learned that you are about to be downsized at work, and your significant other has announced that the relationship is over. What will your prayer be like, assuming you decide to do it at all? Honestly, if it were my situation, I would probably think about some choice words for God and skip the prayer altogether!

If I practice discernment, though, I realize that this attitude tells me about how I presently view God: I'm ready to pray when things are okay but then blame God for any problems that creep up. I try to keep in mind that when I am angry at God, I still need to pray and allow time for God to change me. It's not something I enjoy, but I do it because I trust that in the long run, it will make me more conscious of God's will.

With the help of a guide, one who practices discernment will learn to recognize those movements in prayer that call a person to spiritual growth. But a person may also recognize those factors that truly inhibit spirituality. Just as a good counselor can help a person understand psychological problems, a director can help a person understand when prayer is not the answer to problems. It's important to recognize that there are legitimate blocks to prayer and that for some people, it will be necessary to seek the help of other professionals. Discernment is not a perfect solution to all the things that make life difficult; it is, rather, a specific practice within the context of one's prayer life that can help a person to grow.

To use an analogy, think of discernment as an athlete's physical self-consciousness. One thing I enjoy about rowing in an eight-person boat is that I can become so focused on performing well that I can forget about everything else that's going on in my world. I developed the habit of bringing an almost meditative attention to my form—paying careful attention to every movement of the hands, every stretch of the back, every sensation on the oar handle, every drive with the legs. Over time, I have become able to recognize if something is slightly off: perhaps my hands are a bit too high, perhaps my shoulders are slumping a little, perhaps my timing is out of sync with the other rowers. Usually, I can make small adjustments so that the general feeling in the boat improves. I have, in short, developed a level of self-consciousness that enables me to look for signs that something is wrong. Discernment is like this; over time, people become accustomed to looking for those things that hinder the ability to pray well, so they can seek solutions.

But to take the analogy a step further, imagine that one day a coach is out watching me in the boat and notices that there is a pronounced problem in some aspect of my rowing. The coach, remember, is able to see me in a way that my self-consciousness cannot—he or she can point out problems that may lie outside the scope of my discernment process. Further, sometimes the problems people encounter are not directly related to the activity at hand. If, for example, my coach tells me that my hands are not working smoothly, I might respond that it's because I'm feeling some pain in my wrist. Perhaps it's a minor problem that can be corrected with better form, but perhaps it's due to a medical problem like tendinitis. In the latter case, no amount of discernment on my part will help; I need to seek medical attention. The bottom line is that while discernment is an important practice to bring to the larger picture of the spiritual life, it must be complemented by the understanding that sometimes our spiritual problems are manifestations of problems that need attention outside the realm of prayer.

Ignatius offers several ideas about how to practice discernment that a person can develop more and more over time. The first one involves paying attention to the ways that we make destructive choices in our lives. It's easy to get caught up in choices that bring us only temporary happiness, because our culture is saturated with them. The entertainment industry thrives because we choose them again and again; like candy, they give us a little pleasure for a short time. But candy isn't enough to live on, and so the person who has nothing but candy will, in the long run, be in bad shape. If we get stuck in the pattern of choosing only these temporary pleasures, we can find ourselves unable to get out of the pattern—we become slaves to our unsatiated desire. Our desire, like that of a person who drinks salt water, grows stronger even as we take in what seems to satisfy it.

Under these circumstances, people find that conscience enters the picture. It's often depicted as the angel on the shoulder, telling the person, "Don't eat that chocolate cake! It's bad for you!" Meanwhile, the little devil on the other shoulder says, "Don't listen to that little fairy! Go ahead, live a little!" Not a very good depiction, I must say, since it makes conscience seem like a wet blanket. On a more serious note, people sometimes describe conscience as the part that makes them feel guilty about things, the part that prevents them from really enjoying themselves. It's important to think of conscience as the part of us that discerns the will of God. In other words, when our conscience stings, perhaps it's because God is trying to get our attention. Notice that in this case, the pain of a guilty conscience may be a kind of good pain, calling us to ask questions about the choices we make in life.

As I suggested earlier, though, discernment doesn't happen all at once, and so it is also good to be careful when dealing with guilt. True, sometimes guilt is a call to make different choices about our lives; but other times it may be the result of more deep-seated problems that really are better handled with professional help.

A second idea about discernment applies to people who have decided that they need to make some changes in their lives. Usually, tough decisions, like quitting smoking, take time; people wrestle with the issue before they come to a resolution. There can be obstacles to making a decision, even if a person knows it's the right one. Reasons that to an outside observer seem small can loom large in the mind of the person wrestling with the decision. Discernment under these circumstances is about getting a certain perspective, recognizing that the end result, and not the difficulties along the way, must be a person's focus.

A third key idea about discernment relates to consolation and desolation. Consolation is an increase of faith, hope, and love, giving the person interior peace, while desolation is exactly the opposite. Discernment over the long term is about recognizing how the spiritual life involves both of these at different times and choosing those things in our lives that ultimately lead to more faith, hope, and love.

There is a more positive aspect to discernment. At certain times in our lives, we are faced with more than one good option and have to choose which is the best. I may have to decide whether to go to college or begin work; to get married to someone I love or move to begin a new career; to welcome another child into the family or settle into a permanent lifestyle with the children I already have. In these cases, discernment is not about choosing right from wrong but, rather, about choosing one good over another. These kinds of decisions can be the most difficult precisely because all the options seem good. For Ignatius, the key is the same: which decision allows me to truly become what God is continually creating me to be, in every moment of my life? Which decision makes me most true to myself, the deepest self, where I find God? How do I respond to God's invitation to cooperate in God's constant project of building the real me?

GOD IN ALL THINGS

Developing the practice of spirituality enables one to grow in the ability to see God in all things. Ignatian spirituality is pervaded by this sense of God's presence in all of creation, which means that anything in human experience can be a source for prayer. People unfamiliar with prayer tend to think of it as something you have to do in a church or some other holy place, with hands folded and head bowed. On the contrary, if spirituality is about the ongoing conversation between the person and God, then it can take place at any moment of the day under any circumstances.

The Jesuit poet Gerard Manley Hopkins (1844–89) wrote what I think is the best reflection of this theme, in "God's Grandeur":

> *The world is charged with the grandeur of God.*
> *It will flame out, like shining from shook foil;*
> *It gathers to a greatness, like the ooze of oil*
> *Crushed. Why do men then now not reck his rod?*
> *Generations have trod, have trod, have trod;*
> *And all is seared with trade; bleared, smeared with toil;*
> *And wears man's smudge and shares man's smell: the soil*
> *Is bare now, nor can foot feel, being shod.*
>
> *And for all this, nature is never spent;*
> *There lives the dearest freshness deep down things;*
> *And though the last lights off the black West went*
> *Oh, morning, at the brown brink eastward, springs—*
> *Because the Holy Ghost over the bent*
> *World broods with warm breast and with ah! bright wings.*

I love the image of the Holy Spirit enfolding the world in her wings, caring for it the way that a mother holds her baby close. It speaks of a tenderness that God brings to us, even in the most dismal conditions. Writing during the Industrial Revolution in Great Britain, Hopkins was aware of the difficult conditions in which many people lived at the time. His reference to everything being "seared with trade" points to the way that people can cover up the beauty of creation, immersing ourselves in the commercial world, which can seem so dehumanizing. And yet, he writes, there is still the hint of God everywhere—the "dearest freshness deep down things," as he calls it—suggesting that if we look beyond this world that constantly assaults our senses, we can come to know God's presence.

In Catholic theology, this vision that extends beyond the everyday world toward God is called "sacramental." Developing a sacramental worldview means that we are able to look at the ordinary things in everyday life and ask how God self-reveals through them. To use a personal example, I often marvel at my students, many of whom overcome significant odds in order to attain a college degree. At times, their desire to do well means that they wish to challenge the way I've graded a paper or assignment, and sometimes I have to confront their anger. Under some circumstances, confronting a person's anger makes me defensive: you push, I push back. But I've come to see even expressions of anger as arising out of what I think are very holy desires: a better life for oneself and one's family. So even when a student expresses her anger at me, sometimes I can detect a hint of the work of God moving that student toward her goal.

Seeing God in all things is about challenging the concepts we have formed about God over the course of our lives, recognizing that they are always limited. Part of the way we as human beings think is to break down our world into manageable chunks; we develop a sense of how things work based on what we are able to understand. If God is God, though, our understanding of God will always be very limited. We must be prepared always to challenge what we have previously thought about God and allow God to challenge us to think in a new way. When we allow ourselves this kind of open-eyed wonder at the world, rather than assuming we've got it all figured out, we will begin to be surprised. God will begin showing up everywhere! The English mystic Juliana of Norwich wrote a well-known reflection on a hazelnut, in which she saw the whole of God's creation. This simple little nut became for her a point of insight into God! In our own time, Mother Teresa wrote about how she saw the face of Jesus in the dying poor of Calcutta. These two examples tell us something about the sacramental worldview: *what* we see is less important than the *way* we see it. The whole world can be a moment for discerning God's face, if we are ready to see it.

Too often, it seems, people are looking for God in the big things: great miracles, epic moments, noble causes. We prefer to think of God as the one who parted the Red Sea and did other great deeds. But we do well to think also about the example of Jesus, whose way of manifesting the love of God was simple: one-on-one conversations, oral teaching, compassionate action. He did not always seek the "big things," if we think of them in the political or social sense. What he sought was connectedness to other people in order to teach them about how great God's love for them is. Jesus' God is the God of the story about the prophet Elijah, who looked for God in a strong wind, an earthquake, and fire—but found God instead in a tiny whispering sound (1 Kgs 19:11–13). God shatters our illusions, our concepts, and so if we use them to look for God, then we will be disappointed. But if we simply allow God to self-reveal as God wills, then we will begin to see the hand of God in all things.

To conclude, I am suggesting that if we are to undertake spiritual workouts, we must have a good idea of what to expect. And what Jesus teaches us is that God wants to love us and to be loved in return through the way we love other people in our lives. Our posture in prayer, then, must be one of openness to whatever ways God moves in our lives. We must listen, wait, watch, and be ready for God; we must be vigilant. We must be ready to encounter God in ways that we had not expected, by honestly acknowledging the situations in our lives from which we begin our prayer. We must be ready for correction in order to know the ways we have set up blocks to God in our ways of thinking. We must be prepared to encounter difficulty, both from life circumstances and from our own tendencies toward sin. We must be ready to learn the process of discernment in order that, over time, we may come to find traces of God everywhere.

two beginning
exercises

THE RESOLVE TO UNDERTAKE ANY SERIOUS TRAINING REGIMEN, WHETHER IT
be to simply lose some weight or to prepare for Olympic competition,
first requires that an athlete take stock of his or her level of prepared-
ness. In other words, developing the right habits over the long term
means that we must first assess our ability level. If I want to run a
marathon but can barely walk up a flight of stairs without losing my
breath, then I must take some time just to do some long walks.
Similarly, if we wish to develop a better commitment to prayer, we
must honestly assess where we are in our spiritual lives.

The two exercises described in this chapter can help us in this task. They are useful for anyone, whether a beginner or a regular practitioner of prayer, because they ask us to simply pay attention to the way God is moving us in our daily lives. They can help us to understand where we are starting from so that we can have more realistic expectations of how our conversations with God will unfold over time. My suggestion is that you read this chapter, then spend some time working on these exercises, which can help us assess the state of our spiritual lives. There are a number of questions and meditations I offer throughout the chapter, so use those that you find most useful.

SPIRITUAL AUTOBIOGRAPHY

Ignatius himself does not specifically suggest doing a spiritual autobiography in the text of the *Spiritual Exercises,* but I think he presupposes that those who undertake spiritual workouts will have the kind of self-knowledge that it aims for. He wrote his own spiritual autobiography later in his life, with the help of a companion, reflecting on his own desires to understand and practice the will of God. The work shows the voice of one who has changed over the years and who, with mature reflection, can see his earlier mistakes.

The primary reason for undertaking a spiritual autobiography, written or not, is to assess what factors have had an impact on the way that I respond to God. It is not primarily about fleshing out every detail of life from childhood on. It's simply an attempt to identify the most important events of my life that affect the way I relate to God. More specifically, it involves paying attention to the things that have affected my prayer life: triumphant or traumatic events, the images of God I have developed, important people in my life, successes and failures, hopes and fears, my religious and social education, my abilities and struggles, and so on. By thinking about these things, I can have a more objective understanding of myself. I can look at my past in a new way and ask whether the ways the past has shaped me are best for my long-term well-being.

There was a time when I was coaching high school–age rowers during a summer program. Many were members of crews from their various schools, while others came to try rowing as something new and fun to do in the summer months. I was impressed by the enthusiasm they brought to their practices, and I enjoyed helping them learn. There was one young man, though, whose rowing was simply atrocious. Looking at him from my coaching launch, I began to wonder if perhaps he had some kind of musculoskeletal problem; his strokes were so odd looking that I imagined he was disabled. When he got out of the boat, though, he walked away like anyone else. I tried to coach him for several days, pointing out several things to try, to get him more in sync with the others in the crew, but these corrections made only a small difference. At a certain point, with some exasperation, I asked him where he had learned to row. "I've done some Irish rowing before," he said. Immediately a light bulb went on in my head! Suffice it to say that Irish rowing involves a very different form than what is needed in an eight-person boat. I told him this and suggested that he simply abandon, for the time being, what he had learned in the Irish curragh in order to learn how to row in this different style. He did, and during his next session in the eight, he had no problems.

This story is an example for me of how our prior experiences can strongly affect our present reality. To put it in ordinary language, we all bring "baggage" into our ongoing life experiences. Sometimes this baggage is good and useful—for example, carrying what we learn in school into our work. Other times, however, it can actively hinder us, as in the case I've described. Undertaking a spiritual autobiography is about paying attention to the baggage we bring into prayer, both good and bad, and asking how it affects our prayer life today.

The first known spiritual autobiography by a Christian author is the *Confessions* of St. Augustine, written between 497 and 501. It can be a difficult work for us to read today; however, it not only gives insight into this important figure in Western history but also allows us to see the importance of reflecting on one's past life. At one point, Augustine writes:

You have forgiven and covered up my past sins, blessing me in you and changing my soul by faith and by your sacrament; yet when the confessions of these past sins are read and heard, they rouse up the heart and prevent it from sinking into the sleep of despair and saying, "I cannot." Instead they encourage it to be wakeful in the love of your mercy and the sweetness of your grace.[1]

Here is a man who regrets many of the choices he made earlier in his life and who can look back and see that God has nevertheless forgiven him of all that he has done wrong. Further, he is conscious of how much God has loved him through all of these mistakes, and this consciousness drives him to be more attentive to the ways that God is moving in his life now.

In my mind, Augustine's reflection is indicative of the kind of benefit that spiritual autobiography seeks. In order to see God in all things, we must *want* to see God in all things—we must be ready to acknowledge God not as a judge, or a policeman, or a distant impersonal force, but, rather, as one who is closer to us than we are to ourselves. Unfortunately, all of us develop false images of God over the course of our experiences, and these false images can hinder us from really knowing God. By taking a look at our lives and our experiences, we can come to a clarity similar to that of Augustine. It is worth noting, by the way, that Augustine himself wandered from belief to belief over the course of many years before committing himself to Christian faith, and so his own images of God were (in his retrospect) very skewed. It took a long time and a lot of self-reflection before he could purge himself of all the misunderstandings he had developed as a young adult. We can take comfort in the fact that this towering figure in Christian theology had many doubts, many stops and starts, many steps backward, many misunderstandings in the life of faith. To judge his whole life on the basis of what he did as a young person would be a serious mistake.

Wherever we are spiritually—just beginning to have an interest in the big questions of life or practiced in regular prayer—a spiritual autobiography can help us know ourselves better and thus know better how God has moved in our lives. It need not be a thorough literary work like Augustine's; instead, it might just be a thoughtful reflection on different experiences in our lives. I offer the questions below to get you started:

What have been the high points of your life?
What have been the low points of your life?
Have you ever felt like God was trying to tell you something?
Who are the people that have loved you for who you really are?
What experiences in your life have caused you the most suffering?
What gives you the greatest happiness?
What experiences have most formed the person you are today?
Who have been your heroes?
Who are the people whom you have hated most?
What did you learn about God from your family?
Who in your life is an example of saintliness?
What is most valuable to you?
What is your experience, if any, of religious education?
What have been the most fun experiences in your life?
What are your talents, and how have you used them?

It may be helpful to set aside some time to dwell on those questions you find most thought provoking. It can be good to write your reflections in a journal, because going back to these reflections later can be fruitful and can be the starting point for prayer. What is important is not answering all the questions but, rather, dwelling on those that spark the most thought. As you think about your life, invite God to be part of your memories. The beginning line of one of Ignatius's prayers is "Take, Lord, receive all my memory." When we do this, we ask God to help us become aware of how memories color our awareness of the world and thus our awareness of God's presence in the world. We can ask God to help us look back on our lives in a way that helps us become more thankful for God's presence today.

It is important to remember that the purpose of this exercise is not to relive old problems but to learn about ourselves. (Some may find that painful memories are still too sensitive; if this is the case, then don't dwell on them. Simply acknowledge that they are there, the way a person might take notice of a drama on TV. Eventually, it may become clear that painful memories are the sign of a need for more in-depth counseling.) In order to be honest, we must pay attention to both the positive and negative influences in our lives. With hindsight, we can ask how these positive and negative experiences have shaped who we are today, and in particular, we can ask how they have shaped the way we think about God.

The questions I've listed are just examples of useful ones to ask in thinking about life from a spiritual point of view. You may think of other, more specific questions to ask yourself. The bottom line is that by understanding ourselves more, we can know God more clearly because we can start to recognize the ways that God has been present in our lives even though we may not have been aware of God at the time.

THE *EXAMEN*

A second useful beginning exercise in the spiritual life is the *examen,* which Ignatius himself counseled was the single most important exercise for a person to do every day. In essence, it is about taking a good look at our choices in life and asking whether they have made us better persons. Over time, the *examen* helps us to take regular inventory of our spiritual lives. By praying the *examen,* we become more adept at listening to God and working with God in the ongoing project of building a good life. There are two kinds of *examen.*

The First Type of *Examen*

The first type of *examen* is the kind we undertake when we come to a life stage that makes us think about where we've been—what the previous weeks, months, or years have been like for us. Often, this kind of *examen* happens with some big event, good or bad: graduation, illness, the birth of a child, a family tragedy. Big events in our lives force us to confront the way we've been living and the choices we've made; sometimes we are thankful, and other times we have regrets. When we perform this kind of *examen*, we are asking about how our past attitudes have affected our choices over time.

The Second Type of *Examen*

If the first kind of *examen* is about looking at the scope of our lives, the second kind is about looking more specifically at our consciousness of the past day. It is this practice that becomes the regular maintenance of the spiritual life: it is about paying attention to highs and lows, things we are grateful for and things we regret. In this *examen*, we go through our memories of the day to see what emerges. The following paragraphs explain how to perform this type of *examen*.

1. Pray for Understanding

First, pray that God might help you understand how he is working with you in your everyday life. We choose to risk believing that God is somehow present to us in every moment, and so we pray that in reviewing the day, we may come to know God's activity with us.

2. Give Thanks

Next, recall and give thanks for the good things God has given you. Practice thankfulness for basic goods, like being alive, being with people you love, having food to eat, and so on. The practice of gratitude alone is a valuable exercise for many, particularly those who are at difficult periods in their lives. I came to understand this point recently. Many things in my life seemed to go wrong, and so my spiritual director instructed me to practice this exercise of gratitude. It was the last thing I wanted to do, but I did it. Instead of focusing on all the negative things, I focused on what was good: the love of my family, my health, food, feelings of accomplishment at work, etc. My prayer was simply to thank God for all these and then ask for the grace, the gift, to work toward whatever was on the other side of the difficult time.

3. Pay Attention to Your Feelings

Then pay attention to strong feelings, both positive and negative, that emerge in your recollection of the day. For Ignatius, feelings were a barometer of the spiritual life, for they tell us things about ourselves and our relationship with God. In looking over the past day, ask yourself what feelings were most strong and why. Try not to "censor" your feelings, determining in advance which are permissible and which are not. Simply ask God to help you understand where the feelings come from and what they tell you about your spiritual life.

4. Examine One of Your Feelings

Choose one of the strong feelings from the past day, then dig deeper: let it be the source of your prayer. If this feeling has emerged in your memory of the day, then it surely points to something important. What is it? Is the feeling positive or negative, and how does it move you? Do you want to be angry at God, or do you want to praise God? Whatever the feeling moves you toward can be a source of prayer. Again, remember that honesty and openness are important here. Don't try to predetermine what a prayer should be, any more than you would predetermine what a friendship is supposed to be. Simply allow the feeling to lead you in conversation with God.

5. Look Ahead

Next, move toward looking ahead. As you wind up your prayer from the feeling of the past day, start thinking about how this will affect your choices in the future. Ask God to be with you as you prepare for what lies ahead. Again, pay attention to your feelings: are you looking forward to the next day, or are you afraid of it?

6. Make a Closing Prayer

Close with a standard prayer, like the Our Father, or use some words that connote your willingness to listen to God in the coming day. Again, pray for the grace to discern God's will and the courage to do it.[2]

The *Examen* as a Regular Part of Our Spiritual Life

The *examen* is important for the spiritual life because it is about discerning God's activity in the intimate experiences of my life. Ignatius describes the point in his life where he decided to abandon his wealth and serve the poor, and mentions that he underwent a three-day *examen* and confession! Evidently, the convictions he developed during his convalescence made him very sorry for the choices he had made earlier in life, and so he felt it necessary to make a serious change. Most people, I suspect, don't make such radical conversions; but we all do come to times in our lives when we call into question our earlier choices. The spiritual autobiography can help us come to some clarity about what we've chosen, and so for some, this practice naturally leads into the *examen*. It's almost like reading a story and asking whether you like it or not—when the story is your own life. Even in our day-to-day lives, we can have experiences that make us wonder why we did what we did, and so naturally we do a kind of *examen*.

Developing a habit of doing an *examen* is good spiritual maintenance. It helps us to become more conscious of the ways we make choices in our lives and frees us to be more likely to make choices that are life-giving. Because it is about simply paying attention to our own thoughts, feelings, attitudes, responses, longings, and fears, it is a good spiritual exercise even for people who aren't sure about religion.

But it can also help to make us aware of God in our lives. In traditional Catholic practice, the *examen* is a prerequisite to the sacrament of reconciliation because taking a look at our lives this way enables us to come to a better understanding of our tendencies toward sin. The understanding is that if God wants our ultimate good, then the more our choices match God's will, the more peace-filled our lives become.

It is possible to use the spiritual autobiography as an impetus toward an *examen,* in the first sense of taking a long look at the choices we've made over the course of our lives and seeking to better understand our motivations. It is good, though, to make the *examen* a regular part of our lives, performing it even daily—provided that it does not descend into a kind of scrupulosity that handcuffs our actions and makes us anxious. Again, the point is not to add more and more formality to our lives but, rather, to simply know ourselves better, to know God better. I offer the following reflections, then, for use in regular *examen.*

An *Examen* Can Be Part of Our Everyday Thinking

An *examen* does not always need to be a time set apart. It is good to do this once in a while, really taking stock of ourselves and the choices we've made, but it is also good to integrate elements of *examen* into our everyday thinking. It's possible to do an *examen* while waiting in line, eating lunch, driving, or listening to music. At its most basic level, the *examen* is your response to the question, "What has God been doing in my life?" It is the chance to simply invite God into our consciousness.

By doing an *examen,* a person moves out of the normal flow of everyday experience, so to speak, and turns his or her attention to specific aspects of his or her own life. Most of the time, we are able to let life happen; our awareness of the world is directed outward, toward this and that experience. An *examen* is about turning our awareness inward for a time so that we can ask questions about the way we experience the world. Are we actively creating our lives as we should, or are we passive spectators? Are our choices determined by the people and circumstances around us, or do we create opportunities to live as we are able? Are we responding to God's invitation to live the fullest, most joyful life possible, given the concrete reality of who we are now?

There Is Not a Rigid Set of Rules to Follow

An *examen* is not about following external rules. It is about paying attention to my relationship to God: the ways my personality, strengths, weaknesses, likes and dislikes, choices, and dilemmas tell me about God's movements in my life. It is about asking whether my life over the past day, week, or month has been a manifestation of my most real self, or whether I have somehow shortchanged myself and the people around me by putting up a mask. It may help to pay attention to rules that I consider important, if they help me acknowledge my deepest self; but fundamentally the *examen* is about God moving me toward my greatest freedom.

There is a Gospel story in which Jesus makes an important clarification about religious rules, and I think it applies to other parts of our lives as well. It seems his disciples were being criticized for breaking the society's rules about fasting; some people saw them as failing to pay the proper reverence for the holy day, the Sabbath, by not fasting the same way other people did. Instead of just dismissing the rule altogether, though, Jesus remarks that the Sabbath was made for people, rather than people for the Sabbath (Mk 2:27). In other words, the rules around fasting (or anything else, for that matter) are good only to the extent that they enable people to more fully live out the reality of faith. For many, the rule on fasting was an important part of their religious devotion, and so dismissing it too easily would have undercut their worship. Jesus goes a step further and understands that sometimes rules have the other effect of stifling our creative attempts to live out faith. Rules are important; they connect us with other people in the community and give everyone a chance to act out their faith in concrete ways. But if rules become paralyzing, then they are no longer the right means to the desired end.

An *examen* can help us to look at the ways our lives are governed by rules or attachments, whether they be at the level of family, work, school, church, or society. It can help us to understand, for example, how some rules can actually liberate us to become better people. But it can also help us understand when rules do prevent us from becoming the kind of people God created us to be. Thus the *examen* also involves a kind of discernment. First, we must look at our lives, then discern which elements are good and which are not.

The *Examen* Helps Us Discover Our True Self

The *examen* is about learning about my deepest self and my false selves. We live in a culture in which image often seems more important than substance, where people need to have some kind of recognizable false self in order to fit in. In an *examen,* I try to dig through the layers of image, almost like different levels of paint on an old wall, in order to know what the real me is like. We all know about images—I think everyone has to learn them while in high school, where everyone has to fit into some clique. Unfortunately, cliques, while connecting us to others who share our interests, can often limit the ways we see ourselves. They can give us a sense of identity, but they can also limit our ability to develop a unique one. I am fascinated by the different ways people express their identities today: clothes, body art, activities and hobbies, and other ways. When I look out at the students in my classes, I see all kinds of ways people express themselves. But sometimes I wonder if these same self-expressions become limiting. Do other people base their expectations on the way people look? Do these people limit themselves based on the images they present to the world?

Not long ago, my wife and I refinished a wooden coffee table, and the experience proved to be a metaphor for this tendency to put on false selves. We visited her brother in a small apartment he shared with some fraternity brothers. We were making small talk, when all of a sudden Sue gasped and nearly threw herself onto the floor to look at this beat-up wreck of a table, covered with stains and pizza boxes. After getting over my initial concern that my wife had developed a serious case of lunacy, I asked what in the world she was doing. "It's perfect! Frank, I must have this table!" she said to her brother. It was the typical coffee table one might expect in a fraternity house: not much to look at, but a good place to put pizza. But Sue saw in this table something beautiful. Eventually she made it clear to me that the shape was right because it matched our furniture and because it had rounded ends, which were safer for a home with a toddler. So we brought the table home, and with a great deal of work peeling paint and shelf paper, sanding, and staining, we discovered that it was a truly gorgeous piece of wood underneath the layers of decoration. Today people still remark how beautiful that table is.

It seems to me that many of us are like that coffee table in the state when Sue discovered it. Our beauty has been covered up by the concerns and worries of our lives, and we allow layers of false selves to cover us up. These layers happen, I think, because we want to accommodate whatever seems to be important in the short run: impressing the right people, being thought important, having the right job or car, looking fashionable, whatever. But these short-term priorities don't sustain us. Over time, our real selves become unrecognizable, even to ourselves. The *examen* can give us the kind of vision that sees through the false layers to the reality underneath. The things that are valuable to me today are definitely not the things I thought about ten years ago; but today I am thankful. This teaches me that perhaps the worst thing we can do to ourselves is never to allow God to move our hearts in ways that our false selves react against. We must allow God to be unpredictable because God reaches down to the layer of our most authentic self.

Sometimes the Process Is Uncomfortable

In the process of an *examen,* sometimes we may find ourselves uncomfortable. God has a way of moving us out of our comfort zones, challenging our false selves and encouraging us to live more deeply. This can be scary; it's easy to stay put in life, because that way we never have to be uncomfortable. There will be times when an *examen* makes us confront the ways we make bad choices. I am convinced, though, that this discomfort can sometimes be from God. There have been a number of times in my life when my reaction is "No, no, no!" to whatever possibility looms on the horizon. But with hindsight, I can see that sometimes God is like water, slowly eroding whatever objections my false selves may present. The important question for discernment of these experiences of discomfort is this: will this new possibility enable me to live with greater faith, hope, and love, responding to God's will? Even if the answer is not clear, keeping open the possibility that God is moving me gives me the chance to listen for the ways God may be trying to get my attention. Perhaps God is trying to melt my objections. I have learned to trust that God's plan is better than the ones I concoct, and this enables me to recognize that my objections aren't always justified. I have faith that God will not put me in a life situation I hate but will move my heart to love whatever God asks me to do.

The best example in my recent life has been the choice to adopt children. Early in our marriage, my wife and I were faced with the choice of whether or not to pursue adoption, and it scared me. I was very reticent. Like many, I was clinging to an idea of what a family was supposed to be like—an image I had gained, I suppose, from the typical kinds of family interactions anyone has while growing up. I had images of having children that were "my own" and saw adoption as a second-best option. But I was forced to rethink this view. I met many families with adopted children and came to understand how deeply joyful they were as a result of adopting. I met adults who had themselves been adopted as children, too, and I learned to appreciate their perspective on what it was like to grow up in an adoptive family. I didn't realize it at the time, but in retrospect, I now see that God was moving my heart toward greater freedom—a freedom that has flowered in the decisions to adopt two little girls. Today I can hardly believe I ever reacted against the idea! As I look back, I can see how God slowly helped me to embrace this part of my life, which has brought me such joy.

Change can be hard. It is much easier to look back at a tough period in my life when things have turned out well than to actually be living through a period of suffering. It is possible to put too happy a face on God's will: "Whatever happens, I know God will make me happy." This can be a dangerous position, so let me clarify. Sometimes we suffer. Life events can be unpredictable in both good ways and bad ways, and so to attribute all these experiences to God can make God look like some kind of twisted puppeteer, making us go through suffering for no apparent reason. Over the course of Christian history, many spiritual writers confront this same question about God and suffering and come to a similar conclusion: God does not cause arbitrary suffering. Here is not the place to enter into an extended theological treatment of the question of suffering, so I will focus on the counsel of writers over history whose insights are more profound than any I can offer. God is the one who comforts us in our suffering and enables us to live through suffering. God does will our ultimate good, but the example of Jesus reminds us that even our ultimate good travels through the experience of evil. I love the word that Jesus used in reference to the Holy Spirit: the *paracletos,* the "comforter" or "helper." God is the one who helps us to live in ways that prevent suffering from crushing us, who helps us to make choices that give us life.

The *examen* helps us pay attention to how our choices impel us toward necessary consequences, some of which cause us pain. If I choose to speak angrily, I may hear someone else's anger. If I choose to work too hard, my body may hurt. If I choose to sleep too long, I may be late for an appointment. These are obvious examples of how sometimes negative consequences are simply the outcome of the decisions we make for ourselves, and they point us to one reason why the *examen* can help us to minimize unnecessary stress. Inviting God into our consciousness is about letting God move us toward those choices that are most life-giving, even if they cause us some pain. I think everyone would agree that the most important choices we make in our lives must involve struggle, pain, confusion, and anger; but because we know that the goal is worthwhile, we persevere. In my own life, my choice to marry my wife was something I discerned was good. Of course, no marriage is free from suffering, but in the long run, it is worth it. God promises our ultimate good, and with this in mind, it is possible to see some suffering as part of the journey.

Practical Suggestions for Doing an *Examen*

Here are some practical suggestions for making an *examen,* either by setting aside some time or by integrating reflections into everyday life.

Some Questions

- What has been the most important thing I've done today (this week, this month)?
- How have I been an instrument of God's love toward others?
- Who has shown me God's love? In what way?
- Have I hurt anyone today (this week, this month)?
- Have I treated anyone as a means to an end rather than as a person?

Some Meditations[3]

- Review your day slowly. What stands out? What are you thankful for? What do you regret? What caused you pain? Pay attention to small things, like feeling satisfaction for doing a good job or feeling sorry for missing something important. Pay attention to the memories of the way you felt about things.
- Ask God for the grace to know God's will for your life and to see the ways God is working in your life.
- What do your actions (or failures to act) tell you about your relationship to God? Does anything stand out—a conversation, a time you got angry, something that moved you, an unexpected event, a regret? With patience, ask yourself what your feelings at the time tell you. Did your feelings manifest a willingness to listen to God or to ignore God?

- What patterns do you see over the last day, week, month, or year? What do these patterns tell you about your relationship to God?
- Take your observations into prayer, telling everything to God and asking God for understanding. Allow God to move you—and to surprise you if necessary.

how to get the most out of your workouts

MANY OF THE COLLEGIATE-LEVEL ROWERS I KNOW AT CAMPUSES ALL across the United States are fond of a saying that captures the spirit they bring to their sport: "I can't—I have to row." I see this motto on T-shirts, and I have heard it spoken at many events that rowers might otherwise have enjoyed if they did not have to go to sleep early in order to be on the water by dawn. What people outside the rowing community usually do not understand is why we give up so much, especially in college when there is so much that takes place after hours. The reason is pretty simple: rowers want to win, and morning is the best time to row. But more than that, dawn on a body of water is beautiful; it touches a sense in us that yearns for beauty, making other pursuits seem less important by comparison.

All serious athletes develop a kind of single-mindedness about their sport, such that the rest of their life becomes focused around it. They become much more conscious about the foods they eat, the amount of alcohol they allow themselves to drink, the sufficiency of their rest and relaxation. They must become aware of the things that hinder their ability to get the most out of their workouts, whether those factors be psychological or physiological. In my experience, one of the more difficult psychological barriers to overcome is convincing athletes that training is more important than, for example, partying late at night. Unfortunately, this choice is one that many students don't want to face. With their new freedom living away from home, they don't want to give up what they see as an important part of their college experience. When confronted with this attitude, I have sometimes found myself in the position of having to wax eloquent about the goals we make in life, the kind of person we become through our choices, and the single-minded pursuit of what is good for us. (Trust me, my speech doesn't always work.) But in the back of my mind is always the feeling I so clearly recall of first deciding to train for real. It moves me to be on the water in early autumn as the morning sun slowly dissolves the mist rising from the water, to be stretching out my muscles as they pull me along in the boat. It is this feeling and this memory that help me remember why I love rowing.

Coaching novices is an experience in watching decision making. Invariably, at the beginning of the season, droves of interested people show up wanting to try it out. Over the course of the first few weeks, though, the numbers drop dramatically. Those who came out of a romantic sense of this beautiful sport often find the practical demands too much: training is too hard, they hate waking up early, they find it too time consuming. I understand all of these; the sport is not for everyone. But it helps me to think about what people have to do in order to really do it well. A person can't just show up without being prepared in advance for what is going on. In other words, people have to have an expectation of what will happen on any given day and prepare themselves in advance in order to do it well.

The life founded on prayer must also involve preparation and knowledge of the short- and long-term demands. Many people similarly approach the idea of prayer with romantic notions and good intentions but find the realities of their lives squelching their enthusiasm. I doubt that any endeavor exempts us from having to make choices; prayer, like anything else, means prioritizing. There are hundreds of ways we can spend our time, and so if we are to devote time to prayer, then we must be prepared for what it involves. More than that, though, we must have a sense that what we are doing is worthwhile. It is difficult to remain committed to anything that seems like a waste of time. In the short run, this means trusting those who are already used to doing the activity. Novice athletes trust their coaches and their peers who have been in training for some time, using them as models for where they eventually want to be. Christians trust Jesus and the saints, who are similarly models to follow in their singleminded pursuit of holiness. We need saints—not just those historical figures revered by the church but also those ordinary people in our lives who quietly testify to the work of God in our midst.

People unaccustomed to regular prayer need to be encouraged that the practice is worthwhile, even though, on many occasions, it isn't particularly fun. The examples of Jesus and the saints remind us that seeking God's will always is the source of their joy, even in the midst of terrible suffering. These people show us single-minded devotion to prayer and how the things they do with their lives arise from prayer. For them, prayer is the very lifeblood of their souls; it is what nourishes them to face difficulty and maintain trust in God's ultimate care for them. Prayer pervades every aspect of their lives; their lives become prayer.

Over time, the practices that command our greatest care eventually become the essence of our lives, and prayer is no different. Jesus' life was a constant testament to God; but even Jesus withdrew in important cases to be alone with God. Seeing God in all things can enable us, like Jesus, to make any part of our lives a prayer. But also like Jesus, we must make time for when we must be alone with God. Ignatius understood that in these times, it is important to prepare our hearts and minds for this conversation with God.

In this chapter, I will focus on seven practices: gaining interior peace, practicing the presence of God, making a preparatory prayer, using your imagination, making your requests known, engaging in a closing conversation with God, and repeating what works for you. As you did in chapter 2, read through this chapter to understand what I'm suggesting. Then take some time to practice these suggestions, starting with the most basic one: gaining interior peace. You may want to reread the sections and implement the suggestions I make, if they help. We will return to these seven practices throughout part 2 of the book, so the more comfortable they become now, the more you are likely to get out of the workouts.

GAINING INTERIOR PEACE

If, as in the story of Elijah, God is a "still, small voice," then preparing ourselves for prayer will involve developing the practice of quiet. As I noted in the introduction, this is not easy. I still find it difficult to be quiet; even if there is no outside noise around me, my brain can be overloaded with songs I've heard, clips of recent conversations, lists of things to do, and random thoughts. Perhaps the most significant difference between Ignatius's time and our own is that we confront so much more noise, and as a result it is much more difficult to practice interior peace.

There are many ways one can practice it, though, and so a person can try different things. I suggest that it might be useful to take a long-term approach to prayer and thus spend some time (days, weeks) doing nothing but practicing interior peace. Consider it a "warm-up" exercise, like stretching or even doing a brisk walk—it is not the primary focus of activity, but it is a necessary prerequisite. Just as one cannot immediately run a marathon after sitting for a long time, one cannot dive into prayer and expect mystical experiences to start happening. Here are some practical suggestions; any, all, or none of them might be helpful. Learn for yourself.

- *Change your place.* Go to a park, a church, a quiet room, a garden, an ocean, or anywhere else that frees you from the possibility of distraction. It might help if the place does not carry strong memories that may distract you.
- *Assume a comfortable position.* Prayer does not have to be on your knees! You can sit, stand, lie down, or assume a lotus position. One key, though, is that comfort sometimes means sleep—don't try to practice interior peace if you are exhausted. If you continually find yourself falling asleep when you try this, it may be a sign that you simply need more sleep. On the other hand, though, if you find that this practice is just making you lazy, it may be helpful to try standing up or being in a place with fresh air. The important thing is to find a balance between being uncomfortable and being lazy. I like variety; sometimes sitting works, while other times I just really need to be on a bike, taking in the beauty of nature.
- *Completely relax your body.* Do a survey of all your muscles, starting with your toes and working upward. Pay attention to your shoulders, your neck, your face. These muscles are very often tensed without our realizing it. Use this attention to your muscles to help focus your attention away from all the natural distractions in your mind. If you do get distracted, simply remind yourself to again pay attention to the feeling of your body. If you prefer to be moving, try to pay attention to the good feeling of your muscles working and relax the other parts of your body.
- *Pay attention to your breathing.* Imagine each intake of breath to be a gift given to you by God at that moment, sustaining you, and each exhale to be a way of giving over to God everything in you that is imperfect. Again, you may find distractions creeping in; don't judge yourself, but simply recognize

that they are there and escort your consciousness back to the breathing. It may be helpful to imagine being underwater and that without God's constant gifts of breath you would have no air. Introduce a sense of thankfulness for your breath. When I pray during physical workouts, I feel this. I know that there are many who cannot move in the ways that I can, and so the movement itself becomes a source of great thankfulness.

The point of this exercise in gaining interior peace is to remove the barriers to prayer. If you are easily distracted (as I am), practice not judging yourself for it; this self-judgment can itself be a barrier. Over time, you will find that it takes a shorter time to gain a state of interior peace. Moreover, you may find that at different points during your day, you may want to do this exercise, even in the midst of school or work. The more you learn how to practice interior peace, the more you may want to practice it, for if nothing else, it gives you a chance to relax. Medical studies have shown that this practice is great for reducing stress.

PRACTICING THE PRESENCE OF GOD

Once a person has quieted the mind, it is easier to turn the focus to prayer. Imagine for a moment that you are sitting in a room with your best friend. The TV is on, and you have a book in front of you that you are studying. The phone rings—it's another friend telling you that she's having a hard time trying to find a birthday present for her boyfriend—can you help her think of some ideas? In the middle of the conversation, you remember that your mom's birthday is in two days and that you need to get a card in the mail, then (gosh!) that reminds you that in the mail today was a bill that is past due. Eventually, you hang up the phone and return to studying, but for a moment watch as the scores of today's games flash across the screen.

Imagine, now, that your best friend asks how you're doing. Your answer will probably be pretty much on the surface: "Fine. How are you?" With all the things that have just passed through your mind, it is unlikely that you can immediately pay attention to anything serious, like your fears about not doing well in school, or your concern for the health of your family, or your attitude toward what the future will bring. Gaining interior peace is like getting away from those distractions of the last half-hour and deciding to take your best friend out for coffee. You go out somewhere because you want to make the setting right for a good conversation. But going out isn't enough; now you must actually focus on what your friend is saying by paying full attention.

Practicing the presence of God is paying full attention to the person who is with us always and loves us, but whom we find it easy to ignore because of the demands of our lives. It is a way of just listening. Like a conversation with a friend, though, it will sometimes involve hearing things we don't like to hear. It will lead us through the whole range of our emotions, but it will be something we choose because it is important to us.

The way Ignatius suggests that we really tune ourselves in to God is by praying the Lord's Prayer. For him, this was a particularly powerful prayer, and for many it still is. Try saying it slowly: introduce one word with each inhale, focusing on what it means. "Our"—not mine, not yours, but our; "Father"—loving parent, one who cares, one who seeks our good; and so on. Chew on each word, tasting what it suggests to you about who God is and what God has done in your own life. Pay attention, in a nonjudgmental way; imagine yourself and God about to have a conversation. If it helps, use common words: rather than "Our Father who art in heaven, hallowed be thy name," use "Our Father in heaven, may your name be holy," and so on. By doing this, you make the prayer your own words, rather than the more distant, formal language of liturgy.

You may find other ways to practice the presence of God: perhaps by meditating on some symbol that is meaningful to you or by remembering a particular event in your life for which you are thankful. If you're like me, meditating on the feeling of the movements of the body can be a good way to do this. Again, the method of practicing God's presence is less important than the end result: becoming aware, conscious, of the God who is always with us, but whom we often forget.

MAKING A PREPARATORY PRAYER

You've taken God out for coffee and sat down at the table. Now is the time to say why you've done this. How do you begin the conversation? What do you say to God? An important thing to remember is that a conversation is never just words. It depends on the other person wanting to listen to you and taking the time to be with you. In essence, a conversation has already begun even before words are said. Anyone who has been out on a date with someone knows this. The major hurdle is just getting the other person to be alone with you!

In prayer, God is always the willing listener. We don't have to try to convince God to be with us, because God has already chosen us. We've already cleared the major hurdle! The great nineteenth-century theologian John Henry Newman used a motto that speaks to what we should aim for, then, in conversing with God: "Heart speaks to heart." We can allow ourselves to speak from the heart, to touch the heart of God. We don't need to fuss with the ordinary "small talk" that begins so many of our conversations with other people. The preparatory prayer is our chance to cut to what is most important: telling God that we want our hearts to be aligned with God's heart. It is a chance to say that we want everything in our lives to praise God, or in other words, to be a reflection of what God made us to be. This short prayer can be simply a phrase like "God, I want only what you want" or something similar, but the specific words are less important than the idea they convey: our desire to become free by doing God's will.

By making this preparatory prayer, we remind ourselves of what is most important in our lives. Because so many of us can find prayer time only in the midst of busy lives, it is easy to become distracted from what is valuable. I know that it's easy for me to fall into the trap of not seeing the big picture; I get caught up in whatever crisis is most present. But I am sometimes reminded of a place I used to pass frequently in college that often called to mind the need for putting things in perspective. In the rotunda of Gasson Hall, on the campus of Boston College, are images of Jesuit saints who left their comfortable lives to minister to people in different parts of the world. These pictures are set against stone walls that arch upward, in grand Gothic style, toward the ceiling several stories high. It is an awesome structure, modeled after the cathedrals of Europe and thus designed to impress upon the mind a sense of grandeur, a sense of majesty, a sense of wonder. The symbolism is powerful: the Gothic style was a testament to human creativity and engineering, the very best of the medieval European mind. By contrast, the Jesuit saints left the world that produced this beauty, and went to places like North America, where native peoples lived amidst a sometimes harsh landscape. There are two phrases I remember that are inscribed in this rotunda. The first is the motto of the Society of Jesus: *Ad maiorem dei gloriam,* "To the greater glory of God"—and both the medieval architecture and the stories of the Jesuit missionaries testify to this ideal. The other phrase, though, is vexing: *Quid hoc ad aeternitatem,* "What is this to eternity?"

It is this second phrase that, to this day, captures my imagination. What is anything in our lives when we compare it to eternity? What is a grand cathedral when compared to living in the presence of God? What is the sacrifice of comforts like home and family, to minister to the native people of seventeenth-century Canada, compared to living in the house of the Lord forever? What is the importance of this work, this concern, this issue, compared to the reality of our lives before God?

I do not mean to suggest with these reflections that our lives or our problems are unimportant. Rather, I mean to suggest that reflecting on the big picture can help us to gain some perspective and to pay attention to what is most important in our lives. When we speak to God in prayer, we speak to one who knows us better than we know ourselves. God already knows the struggles we face, the hopes and fears we have, the sins we fall prey to, our desire for goodness. Understanding this allows us to be completely honest with God and hence with ourselves. It can help us to make the preparatory prayer a testament to our own dependence on God for spiritual sustenance, for centeredness, for meaning. In this way, the prayer becomes a way to cleanse our hearts of anything that is not of God or, better, a way to ask that God cleanse our hearts so that we may know God and God's will more clearly and thus be liberated by it.

USING YOUR IMAGINATION

Perhaps the most basic and practical of Ignatius's ideas about prayer is his suggestion that we use our imagination. One example of this practice is what he calls "composition of place," indicating that it is about using our minds to put together a picture of what our prayer is about. There are two possibilities. The first is the more obvious: we read a scriptural story and imagine that we are part of that story, applying our senses to give us a very realistic idea of what the story is about. The second possibility takes a little creativity; it involves coming up with some image of an abstract idea like thankfulness or sin or dependence. In both cases, though, the idea is to make prayer time an exercise in imagination so that during and after the prayer, we can pay attention to the ways we imagine God in our lives.

The imagination is a powerful tool. Sports psychologists have begun to use the power of imagination to enhance athletic performance by encouraging athletes to visualize themselves in the midst of their activity. When I was a coach, I always spent time with my athletes, practicing this exercise. I spent perhaps twenty minutes having them imagine their race the following day, a race that usually lasted only about six or seven minutes. They imagined the start of the race, carefully breaking down each initial stroke, so key to establishing a rhythm early on. They focused on their breathing, their hands on the oar, their posture, their leg drive. I wanted them to break down every element of their stroke, to focus their attention on what it feels like to row well, even though it all happens at once in a matter of seconds. I asked them to feel themselves relaxed and rowing well, to imagine a boat in perfect synchronicity being lifted off the water and speeding smoothly through the course.

Sometimes what emerged during these exercises was someone's concern about a particular part of the race, perhaps one that had been troublesome over the course of training the week before. In other words, the imagination exercise, when reflected upon later, highlighted something that the athlete needed to be particularly conscious of during the race. Usually, I found, this heightened consciousness enabled the athlete to execute well whatever concerned him or her. It helped the person to understand what part of the race needed specific attention.

This is a helpful metaphor for what using imagination in prayer helps us to do. By bringing imagination to bear on a particular aspect of our spiritual lives, we come to better understand what struggles we face, what issues we have yet to resolve, what ways God is calling us to grow. It is a very straightforward way of paying attention to our deeper selves, which often get overlooked in our busy lives. For while our spirituality is always underneath the layers of consciousness we use in everyday life, it often remains hidden. We tend to act out the symptoms of our spiritual selves, and if this aspect of ourselves is hurt, we can tend to behave in ways that do not further our ultimate good. The exercise of imagination in prayer makes us pay attention to our spiritual core and to the ways we manifest the character of this core in our choices.

There was a time when I learned something important about myself by using this kind of prayer. I was meditating on the story of Jesus feeding the five thousand—the story in which Jesus takes a few loaves and fishes and is able to feed the hordes that had gathered to listen to him. This was a story I had heard many times; I did not expect anything different to happen in my prayer. But I went ahead anyway, reading the story very closely and expecting to feel the usual sort of interest: it was nice that Jesus could do that for those people, etc. But as I read closely, a phrase caught my attention in a way I don't think I had ever even heard it before. It jumped out at me so that I could barely believe that I had missed it before. After the disciples ask Jesus to send the massive crowd home so they can buy food before too late, Jesus says, "You give them something to eat" (Mk 6:37).

Imagining the scene, I saw Jesus looking straight at me, emphasizing the "*You* give them," suggesting to me something of Jesus' expectation that I be the one to do something. In my prayer, I was a little uneasy, even perhaps a bit indignant: "You're Jesus (for God's sake!); you do it!" But I was on the spot. In fact, the rest of the story started to fade into the background of my imagination. In the story, Jesus eventually asks the disciples to gather the available food (five loaves and two fish), after which he prays to God, then distributes it to all five thousand. I was stuck on the image of Jesus looking to me to feed these people.

What this exercise taught me about was how I envisioned myself in relation to God: God was supposed to take care of everything while I sat and watched. After this prayer, though, I began to question the legitimacy of this image. It was clear that my imagination was getting stuck on a problem: the fact that Jesus wanted me to do the feeding told me that I needed to be more aware of the ways that I minister to other people, rather than just assuming God would put everything in order. As I think back on this exercise now, I am aware of how it has made an effect on the way I think about the world. I don't understand God's ways in the world, but I am convinced that I and others are called to do God's loving work wherever we can. It seems to me that many problems we face as a society are due to our failures to love as Jesus did; and if we continually blame God for the messes we find ourselves in, we may ignore our own responsibilities for solving them (and for creating them in the first place). I still get mad at God and question the ways God made things, but now I know that I cannot ignore my responsibility to do the work of loving when I can.

As noted earlier, imagining oneself in a story is simple: What do you see? Smell? Hear? Feel? Taste? The more specific the senses, the more vivid the imagination. It can be helpful to dwell on each of these senses for some time, drawing out the time frame of the images the way I asked my athletes to do. There may be insights anywhere along the way, so it is good not to rush through. In fact, it may be helpful to imagine the same scene several times, to return to fruitful images. In chapters 4 through 6, I will offer some stories that are good for this imagination exercise. If you find that one of the stories is particularly helpful, return to it at different points in the same day, week, month, or year—it can be good to revisit stories that challenge us to spiritual growth, even if only to understand later how we have changed.

The first method of using imagination in a scriptural story is something anyone can do—especially children, who love to use their imagination. The second method, though, can be more difficult; for instead of presenting us with the scene into which we insert our imagined selves, it demands that we come up with the appropriate image. Our selection of the image, though, can itself tell us a great deal about our spiritual selves, for the image will have to come from something in our experience. To use an important but difficult example, what image comes to mind when you conceive of sin? Do you imagine some historical event, like the Holocaust, or an injustice you saw performed by someone else, or some injury done to you, or something you have done? What does this image selection tell you about how you think about sin?

A literary example may illustrate how this application of imagination can be helpful. In Dante's fourteenth-century epic *The Divine Comedy*, he begins with an observation about his own spiritual life:

> *In the middle of the journey of our life*
> *I found myself astray in a dark wood*
> *Where the straight road had been lost sight of.*[1]

The entire epic is Dante's creative reflection on the state of his soul, which he imagines here as being lost in a dark forest. For Dante, this image of losing one's way is a metaphor for this moment in the spiritual life. As one progresses through his story, it is easy to be struck by how detailed is his imagination of hell, purgatory, and heaven. Dante is able to convey his understanding of the spiritual life through different images and events of this journey.

Most of us will never have the chance to create such an extended vision of our spiritual lives, but we can follow Dante's lead and use our imagination to understand them. If you conceive of your life as a journey, where are you now? Are you in the fast lane? Broken down on the side of the highway? On cruise control? At a rest stop? Stuck behind a slow-moving vehicle? Are you preparing for the next stage of the journey by packing your bags? Have you just had a major accident? These are all images that we today can use to consider where we are in our lives, and there are many others. What kind of journey are you on? Where are you going? What kind of transportation are you using—car, plane, bicycle, feet? Who are your companions? How long do you think they will be with you? What kind of map are you using, if any? How has the journey been so far? Are you lost? Whom have you asked for directions?

These questions are suggestions for imagination. It is useful to consider your own questions, too, by paying attention to the things that happen as you imagine what your life looks like. In prayer, imagination can help us pay attention to things that we have not, perhaps, previously considered. It can tune us in to details and make us reconsider the ways we have become accustomed to thinking about things. In my example above, Jesus' words to me became the central focus of my prayer. Those words were always in the text, but I had not paid attention to them until I used my imagination.

In my classes, I usually do a short exercise with my students that helps them to recognize something about the way we think about the world. After talking for a few minutes, I tell them to close their eyes and think about what the classroom looks like. Then I begin to ask very specific questions about things that were in their field of vision but that many have not really paid attention to: What color is the floor? What is on the sign above the blackboard? What color shirt am I wearing? By asking these specific questions, I am asking them to pay attention to the ways that they use their vision. With every question, I find that only a handful of students can correctly identify the answers, meaning that although these items were in their field of vision, many students did not really pay attention to them.

It seems to me that this exercise is a metaphor for the way we operate in life. At any given moment, there are countless things we can look at in our field of vision—or to put it another way, in our field of vision, there are too many things to really pay attention to. We exercise a selective attention, meaning that we tend to focus on what we think is most important—the person in the room, rather than the color of the furniture; the car in front of us, rather than the spelling on the road signs; the words on the page, rather than the table the book is resting on. Our minds work in such a way that certain things need to be in the foreground, others in the background. And what is true for our vision is also true of our thinking. We tend to focus on what we think is most important. So when we use imagination in thinking about biblical stories, we give ourselves the chance to change our focus. Imagination gives us control over the stories: we can freeze the action, rewind, fast-forward, skip, or whatever, so we can pay attention to both the foreground and the background. What is key is that sometimes the background is more important. It comprises all those elements that we do not perceive to be as important but that perhaps we should consider. I will use one of the gospel stories to illustrate this point.

The story of Zacchaeus is about a man who climbs a tree to get a good look at Jesus (Lk 19:1–10). Zacchaeus is small, and there is a great crowd around Jesus; so Zacchaeus decides that this is the only way he will ever get a chance to see this person everyone's talking about. In the story, Jesus spots Zacchaeus in the tree and says to him that he will stay with him; others criticize Jesus for staying with someone who is regarded as a sinner because he collects taxes.

It's an interesting story, but there is not much detail. When I imagine this story, I try to picture what it would be like as the different characters: Jesus, Zacchaeus, a member of the crowd. With these different perspectives, I can get a better sense of what might have actually happened. Luke gives us only a sketch in order to put into the foreground Jesus' decision to stay with a sinner, to "save what was lost" (Lk 19:10 NAB). This is an important theme, no doubt, but I don't think it's the only one. What's in the background? What strikes me is Jesus' decision—he ignores the people who have gathered around him. I think about how it's likely that there were some men who left work to meet him and probably traveled to get there. There might have been some women trying to keep their children in line as they walked from their homes to meet this public figure.

These were people who were interested in hearing Jesus—why did he ignore them? If I were a member of the crowd, I would probably feel a little resentful. If Zacchaeus had to climb a tree, maybe it's because he got there late or because he just happened to show up and was curious. Why did Jesus talk to him rather than to the people who took the time to get there earlier? On the other hand, though, I think about Zacchaeus himself, perhaps legitimately wanting to meet the holy man he's heard about but feeling left out because he's short. Maybe climbing a tree was the only way he could really see Jesus because the people closer to him were being selfish. Maybe Jesus himself could recognize that the crowd was a group of publicity hounds, and like some in the media today, they were there only because there was a story. Maybe Jesus called Zacchaeus because Jesus himself was paying attention to the background and not just to the people in the foreground.

Applying imagination to this story enables me to consider many different scenarios and to focus on different elements. When I do this, I am able to think about it in a richer way and to draw from it interesting conclusions about how I look at Jesus and his followers. I am able to bring the background into the foreground and pay greater attention to it, to see what I can learn from it. And I can ask God to help me understand what God wants.

MAKING YOUR REQUESTS KNOWN

Imagination can help us to set the stage for prayer, and it can itself be a prayerful exercise. But imagination can be tricky since it doesn't have to obey any laws. I often find my imagination flying off track; one minute Zacchaeus is in the tree, and the next he has sprouted wings and flown above the crowd, dropping water balloons on people. So an important complement to the practice of imaginative prayer is asking God for what we want out of it—making our requests known to God (who already knows) and to ourselves (who don't always really know). This means that we are dwelling on a particular aspect of the spiritual life that we need to consider, so that we can have a sense of how to proceed in our prayer.

It is helpful to consider that while prayer is ultimately about making our lives reflect what God wills for us, our limitations make us able to progress slowly. As I've already suggested, we must develop a long-term approach to prayer, or any endeavor that is worth pursuing, and be prepared to move one step at a time.

One of my favorite exercises in coaching rowing is the preparation for the start of an upcoming sprint race. Athletes are usually excited and pumped up for a competition, and if the race is only a few days away, they tend to be very motivated. So working on starts can be very exciting because it helps us to think about actually being in a race situation. The start is important; it involves five initial strokes that can set the tone of the whole race. And while a race may involve upwards of two hundred strokes, the first five can be critical—we can spend hours of practice on just those first five strokes. In fact, I have sometimes spent half an hour just working on the very first stroke! I have to remind my athletes to pay attention to many different elements: their hands, their posture, their leg drive, the depth of the oar, the synchronicity with other members of the crew, and so on. It takes patience and perseverance to get that first stroke right, then to move on to practice the first two strokes. The point is that no one can immediately do perfect starts without first practicing individual strokes, and no one can row perfect races without paying specific attention to the different elements in the race.

Developing a prayer-filled life in response to God's will involves no less attention to the different elements of our lives. When we articulate for ourselves our intentions in prayer, we put ourselves in the position of focusing in on one particular aspect. We tell God what we hope to do in prayer and also ask that God help us to achieve what will help us to grow as persons. Making our requests known is analogous to identifying the particular purpose of a workout session. I can't become a completely fit person unless I spend certain days working on my legs, other days working on my cardiovascular fitness, other days working on my arms, or back, or chest; I can't become a good basketball player unless I work on my dribbling, passing, and shoot-ing; I can't become a good golfer unless I work on different kinds of shots. No one can develop a good prayer life unless he or she takes the time to work on all the different elements in prayer—and these ele-ments, by the way, are as diverse as the experiences in our lives. So making our requests known is about seeking to connect our prayer to the problems of our everyday lives by paying special attention to one thing at a time.

Returning to the image of taking God out for coffee, I suggest that when we make our requests known, we begin with a particular topic of the day's conversation. I cannot be a friend to someone except through the process of daily interaction with that person. I cannot suddenly do "friendship" with anyone; I can talk with someone, go to a movie with someone, help someone through a problem, have tea with someone—and through doing these things, establish a friend-ship. Notice that these activities, though, will involve some level of communication, and even that doesn't just happen in a vacuum. I don't just "communicate"—I talk about sports, the weather, the news, problems; I laugh with my friend; I share a task with him or her; I send e-mail back and forth. In order to do prayer, then, I similarly must have something to begin with. I thank God for good things; I ask God for help; I cry to God in pain; I praise God for all that is mysterious; I listen to God for guidance. When we make our requests known, we pay attention to what is going on around us and ask that God move our hearts to better understand how to live our lives according to God's will.

In the Spiritual Exercises, there are four major themes that emerge over the four weeks, and these themes provide the framework for our conversations with God. First, we pay attention to how the mistakes we've made in life prevent us from being the best persons we can be. The requests in this first week, then, center around the question, "How have I alienated you, God?" Second, we focus in on how we are confronted with the choice of living with Christ or not, and thus our requests will relate to knowing Christ more closely. Third, we look at the consequence of being like Christ: for if his life led to the cross, we ask for understanding of why he did this for us. Fourth, we meditate on Christ's resurrection from the dead and ask that we come to know the joy of new life. There is, then, a progression through these exercises: by meditating deeply upon the life of Christ, we can come to more carefully model our own lives after his and thus imitate his radical faithfulness to the will of God.

ENGAGING IN A CLOSING CONVERSATION WITH GOD

For Ignatius, the closing conversation was the proper way to end the time of prayer with God. The etymology of the word *conversation* is helpful: it comes from Latin roots meaning "turning together." It suggests that in prayer, the praying person undertakes a movement with God, almost like passengers in a car. The image in the coffee shop reflects this understanding of prayer.

I think that Ignatius, when he suggests that we close our prayer by conversing with God, already understands that the whole of prayer time is conversation. But he is more specific: after directing us to gain interior peace, practice the presence of God, make a preparatory prayer, use our imagination, and make our requests known, he directs us to simply talk to God about what has just happened. There is nothing complex here; we should just be ourselves and speak from our hearts to God about what the prayer session was like. Perhaps one way to think about this direction is to consider prayer something that God and you undertake together, and the closing conversation as the chance to talk about it together afterward. I imagine this as what happens on the ride home from the coffee place, or the talk between friends after seeing a game together, or maybe even the processing of a shared experience of something painful, after the fact. This is also an imaginative exercise, of course, and so it will involve much of the same kind of activity described above. Ignatius even suggests that we engage other characters in the biblical stories in this closing conversation on certain occasions as a way of helping ourselves understand the meaning of the prayer time.

Think of a time you needed to have a serious conversation with someone. Most of the time, we speak to our friends in everyday language. If we really need to talk about something serious, we have to prepare that person: "We need to talk. Can we go somewhere?" The conversation unfolds; you spill your guts to the person; you listen closely; you laugh or cry together; you hopefully come to some shared understanding. When a point of resolution finally comes, you close the conversation: "Thanks for taking the time to be with me. I'm so glad we had a chance to talk about this. It's been on my mind for a while, and I needed to let you know what I've been thinking." This, of course, is an optimistic example, but the point is that the tenor of the conversation can change when the main subject has already been addressed. The "conversation" may be over, but the two may keep talking. When we undertake a time of prayer, there is a main theme; the closing conversation allows us time to then think about what was going on as we meditated upon that theme. It gives us the chance to almost step outside ourselves for a moment, to take a look at how we have changed as a result of praying. It is about letting God help us to see ourselves.

One metaphor that sticks in my mind as I consider the closing conversation is that of reviewing video of a practice. In any sport, watching video of one's own performance can be enlightening because it is impossible to get an objective view of oneself. What I cannot feel I am doing wrong I may be able to see, if I am shown a video. Or seeing the way I perform may help me realize that I am not as bad as I may think. Another metaphor is a theatrical rehearsal in which I take part as an actor. I play my part, say my lines (perhaps with some improvisation!), and really imagine myself as the character in the play. At the end of the scene, I talk with the director and the other actors about how the scene went and analyze the ways I felt as it was happening. In both examples, the closing conversation is an integral part of the experience (training or acting), and it helps a person have a better understanding of how to do it well.

REPEATING WHAT WORKS FOR YOU

In several places, Ignatius suggests that people undertaking his Spiritual Exercises return to a text they used earlier in their prayer. Repetition can be an important spiritual practice; it gives people the chance to reexamine the ways they have been moved in prayer. The rule of thumb is that there is no specific formula in prayer: use what works. If you have been particularly moved by using a specific text, use it again. This does not always mean that a person should always return to texts that made her feel happy. On the contrary, sometimes those texts that move us the most induce feelings of sorrow. The point is not to rush through anything; we don't graduate from the workouts like we graduate from high school or basic training. The practice of repetition in prayer is about returning to a fruitful topic of conversation between you and God.

The old joke about Carnegie Hall gets to the point:

TOURIST: *How do you get to Carnegie Hall?*
NEW YORKER: *Practice, practice, practice!*

In order to do anything well, prayer included, we must practice. Repetition ingrains in our minds the practice so that it becomes habitual. We seldom get anything new the first time around; but after repetition, it becomes second nature. Actors repeat their lines over and over; basketball players repeat shots thousands of times over their lives; baseball players take batting practice before every game. And praying people repeat prayers many times so that they become part of the fabric of their worldview. Repetition is not an end in itself but, rather, the means to the greater end of spiritual insight. Sometimes, we "get it" only after repeating it many times. My example of prayer using the story of Jesus feeding the five thousand illustrates this point. The practice of repetition allowed me to pay attention to something I had not previously seen.

I wish I could say that the more one prays, the easier it becomes. In one sense, this may be true, for one comes to a better understanding of one's own habits, shortcomings, and needs. But in another sense, prayer can help us to become aware of how little we really know God. Just as good athletes become aware of how much they need to improve, or scholars learn how much they don't understand, or saints come to understand how much they need to grow in holiness, so, too, do praying people learn how hard it can be to truly know the will of God. But the difference is that regular prayer is itself the work of trying to become better, as is regular training or regular study. Perfection, whether it be athletic or academic or spiritual, may be out of reach, but we are better for at least moving ourselves in the right direction. Using the seven practices in prayer will help us to develop a habit of seeking to know God.

4

the foundation

NOT LONG AGO, MY SISTER MOLLY MADE AN IMPORTANT DECISION IN HER life: to join the U.S. Marines. She visited a recruiter, learned about the various branches of service, and decided on her plan of action. In the late summer, she added her name to the list of recruits and was told that she would begin basic training in the spring. In the meantime, the recruiter told her, she should get as physically fit as possible.

She began running in order to develop a good cardiovascular base. She lifted weights, swam, rode a bike, played ultimate Frisbee, and went rock climbing. She was very dedicated and got into shape so she could be ready by spring to take on the rigors of full-time marine training. She ended up graduating at the top of her company.

Ignatius, being a military man himself, would have approved of Molly's preparation. He understood that a serious training regimen depends on a person's developing a strong foundation, both mental and physical. And so when in his *Spiritual Exercises* he offers a "Principle and Foundation," he gives us a look at the kind of relationship one must cultivate with God in order to grow spiritually. Now that we've looked at some practices to help us in prayer, it is time to explore where they should lead us.

In the rest of this chapter, I'll discuss the principles, which comprise the foundation for a healthy faith. Along with the discussions of the principles, there are several spiritual exercises, each of which includes one or more scriptural texts for use in prayer. In doing a particular exercise, it may be best to read through my reflections first, then to go back to the text to pray using the seven practices described in the previous chapter:

1. Gaining interior peace.
2. Practicing the presence of God.
3. Making a preparatory prayer. (In this case, pray that God might help you to understand the things in your life that hinder you from knowing God's will.)
4. Using your imagination. (Put yourself in the story, and use all your senses.)
5. Making your requests known. (Let God know what you are thinking about.)
6. Engaging in a closing conversation with God.
7. Repeating what works for you.

Read through this chapter, then spend some time praying the texts that help us come to appreciate the principles of authentic prayer.

THE FIRST PRINCIPLE:
BUILDING OUR LIVES ON PRAISE, REVERENCE, AND SERVICE

Principle 1. We are created to praise, reverence, and serve God our Lord, and by these means to achieve our eternal well-being.

This first principle is a disarmingly simple statement about the meaning of life, but because of this, it demands a second look. The implication, I think, is that if we are to build our lives on prayer, then this must be the principle upon which we build them. It's straightforward enough, but it forces us to ask some basic questions: Do I live this belief? What would my life—my day-to-day choices—look like if I honestly believed this principle? If my life were really founded on the belief that I was created by God for praise, reverence, and service, then it would seem that everything I do must somehow be related to these goals. Is this the case?

Take a few minutes to do an *examen* of the past day. What stands out in your memory? What were the highs and lows? What were the challenges and rewards? How was God present to you, even if you weren't aware of it? Now, ask yourself: Did my life over the past twenty-four hours manifest a pursuit of my eternal well-being? Did my actions and choices show praise, reverence, and service of God? What *really* has been the source of my motivation?

It can sometimes be enormously difficult to understand why we do the things we do. Addressing this inner conflict we all face, St. Paul wrote, "I do not understand my own actions. For I do not do what I want, but I do the very thing I hate" (Rom 7:15). The first principle can act as a knife to cut through the layers of our false selves to get to the core. Human beings are complex; Ignatius knew this, and modern psychology has illustrated this point even further. By paying attention to this first principle, we allow ourselves to confront the reality of ourselves that we often ignore. The grim truth is that there are parts of ourselves that we do not wish to confront; they remain hidden behind the elaborate façades we manage to create for the world.

The well-known tale of the emperor's new clothes speaks to some of the ways we can deceive ourselves. The story is about an emperor who hires a tailor to make him some new clothes for an important event. The tailor tells the emperor that he will use the finest, most expensive threads for this garment, and the emperor promises to reward him richly. After some time, the tailor returns with this garment, which, he says, is of cloth spun so fine that it cannot even be seen. The emperor, believing him, puts on the garment to the praise of his court. All of his subjects, fearing to tell him the truth that he is wearing nothing at all, continue to compliment him on his fine raiment. Eventually, though, a little child calls a spade a spade and says to the emperor, "You're naked!"

The story suggests to me that we can all act like emperors of our own little empires, receiving the false message that we are all perfect in every way and that surely people as good looking and intelligent as ourselves must want the latest things that money can buy! Our culture often sends us messages that all is well if we simply have the emperor's new clothes, whatever they may be. Ours is a culture of achievement: we must get the right grades in school, the right degrees, the right jobs, the right relationships, the right bodies, the right possessions, and the list goes on. And we, as a result, convince ourselves either that we are good because we have these achievements or that we are failures because we do not.

Living the practice of the foundation is about challenging the false notions that tell us what is good and bad in life. It is about recognizing that God is good and that because God is good, we, as God's creations, are also good. It is about further recognizing that even though we are good, we sometimes make choices that diminish us. It is about challenging our dominant cultural worldview, the one that we have come to embrace in an unfree way because of the culture in which we live. It is about turning in full freedom to seek the will of someone who knows our ultimate good better than we do, in order that we might achieve the end for which God created us.

Exercise on
Seeing Ourselves As God Does

Use the following two texts in prayer for several days:

God created man in his own image, in the image of God he created him; male and female he created them. . . . And God saw everything that he had made, and behold, it was very good. (Gn 1:27–31)

[Jesus said,] "You, therefore, must be perfect, as your heavenly Father is perfect." (Mt 5:48)

The first message is good news: our truest, deepest selves were created by God simply for God's own delight in creating us. Each human being is a unique work of art; God throws away the mold after making each one of us. What this suggests, then, is that our lives have unique ways of praising, reverencing, and serving God—even when we are unaware that we are doing it. I marvel at the array of talents and lifestyles out there, especially those that are completely foreign to me, because they remind me of how varied are the ways that people can praise God. Some people praise God through their friendships; others through their art; others through their perseverance; others through their work. In short, when we are most ourselves, doing what we are capable of doing, we are praising God.

To praise, reverence, and serve God is to achieve our perfection as human beings. Jesus' command is difficult, though: no one is perfect. And so immediately we must recognize that Jesus is not calling us to some antiseptic kind of life, in which we are afraid to do anything for fear of failure. Rather, he is calling us to understand that by our very humanness, we are capable of being loved by God and thus capable of loving as God loves. The quote above about being perfect comes after Jesus' command to love our enemies, suggesting that our perfection lies precisely in our ability to mirror the kind of love that God has for all of us.

There is nothing we must do in order to be loved by God. There is nothing we must achieve, nothing we must change, nothing we must seek before God loves us; it is already an accomplished fact because God created us in order to love us. Our perfection is simply our desire to respond to this already accomplished fact, to make our lives great because we are capable of it.

Exercise on Seeing God as God

Perhaps the most fundamental challenge people face in their spiritual growth is seeing God as God—the one who has created each person in God's own image, and who cooperates with us every moment as we create our lives. In this exercise, we pray for the grace to recognize God as the author and co-creator of our very selves.

> *Hear, O Israel: The LORD our God is one LORD; and you shall love the LORD your God with all your heart, and with all your soul, and with all your might. And these words which I command you this day shall be upon your heart; and you shall teach them diligently to your children, and shall talk of them when you sit in your house, and when you walk by the way, and when you lie down, and when you rise. (Dt 6:4–7)*

To praise, reverence, and serve God our Lord means to work with God at each moment, constructing our lives in such a way that all our choices, all our desires, all our hopes are oriented toward the love of God. In other words, our happiness depends upon loving God with all our heart, soul, and strength. Take some time to consider how you do this, even when you aren't thinking about it.

THE SECOND PRINCIPLE: FOCUSING ON OUR ETERNAL WELL-BEING

Principle 2. Everything in the world is to help us toward our eternal well-being. If something helps us, we should use it; and if it hinders us, we shouldn't.

This is the principle of openness. Remember that the fundamental idea is that if we've got our eyes on the goal, then how we get there becomes less important. When sports commentators talk about a team who has played terribly but managed to get a few lucky breaks to win a game, they often say something to the effect that "it all looks the same in the box score"; that is, in the newspaper the next day, it doesn't matter whether you played brilliantly or badly—you still get one in the win column. Here Ignatius suggests that life in general is like that: a person might be a king or a homeless person, but in eternity it makes little difference.

Exercise on Seeing the World As God Does

Use several days of prayer to consider the story of Lazarus and the rich man, which Jesus uses to say something about this fundamental principle. It's a story that is ripe for imagination.

There was a rich man, who was clothed in purple and fine linen and who feasted sumptuously every day. And at his gate lay a poor man named Lazarus, full of sores, who desired to be fed with what fell from the rich man's table; moreover the dogs came and licked his sores. The poor man died and was carried by the angels to Abraham's bosom. The rich man also died and was buried; and in Hades, being in torment, he lifted up his eyes, and saw Abraham far off and Lazarus in his bosom. And he

called out, "Father Abraham, have mercy upon me, and send
Lazarus to dip the end of his finger in water and cool my tongue;
for I am in anguish in this flame." But Abraham said, "Son,
remember that you in your lifetime received your good things,
and Lazarus in like manner evil things; but now he is comforted
here, and you are in anguish. And besides all this, between us
and you a great chasm has been fixed, in order that those who
would pass from here to you may not be able, and none may cross
from there to us." (Lk 16:19–26)

Focus on the image of the rich man. What in your life makes you rich? What do you most value? What things in your life make you happy? What things in your life hinder you from being more loving? It is interesting to note that this meditation may work both ways: helping you to see things you value too much and helping you to see things you do not value enough. The objective is not to suggest that money, fame, popularity, or other things are bad but, rather, to suggest that ultimately they are good only to the extent that they help us achieve our eternal well-being. Pay attention to your imagination: What do you feel when you, the rich man, see Lazarus? What does it feel like to wear fine linen while Lazarus is in rags? Apply your senses to the scene, and see what happens.

Next, focus on the image of Lazarus. Who is a Lazarus in your life? In what ways are you a Lazarus? Put yourself in the story. What do you, Lazarus, see around you? What do you feel like? What is it like to see the rich man when you are so needy? What is it like to feel so hungry that you envy the rich man's dogs? What do you feel when the dogs come and lick your sores?

Finally, put yourself in the place of each man after death. What does it feel like to look back on your life as a rich man? As Lazarus? What do these feelings tell you about your attitude toward death? Toward the priorities you make in life today?

THE THIRD PRINCIPLE: PUTTING ASIDE OUR CONCERN FOR THE EXTERNALS

Principle 3. We must not care about external things, like health or sickness, wealth or poverty, fame or obscurity, a long life or a short one.

In Jesus' time, many people believed that sickness and family tragedies were the result of being cursed by God as a sinner. Today some people still hold to this belief. Ignatius challenges us to consider things in a different way: all experiences in our lives, whether joyful or painful, can be occasions of grace, God's gift of self.

Exercise on Seeing People the Way Jesus Did

Jesus did not judge people according to the cultural standards prevalent at the time. Instead, he sought to see each human being as a unique creation of God. In this exercise, we pray for the grace to see people in the same way.

As he passed by, he saw a man blind from his birth. And his disciples asked him, "Rabbi, who sinned, this man or his parents, that he was born blind?" Jesus answered, "It was not that this man sinned, or his parents, but that the works of God might be made manifest in him." (Jn 9:1–3)

Jesus wanted to show in this and other examples that our notions about God can often be mistaken. Sometimes, it seems, God can be most present to us when we are suffering. Paradoxically, though, it is during these times of suffering that God can seem most absent, and so Ignatius asks us to pay attention to the fact that suffering may indeed be a place where we can come to know God's will. This is not to say that we should go out looking for it; rather, it is to say that when it (inevitably) comes, we need not think that it means God has abandoned us.

It is important to remember that Jesus, too, felt abandoned by God on the cross; feeling the absence of God is part of the spiritual life. What is important, though, is maintaining faith even in these periods when we feel abandoned. We are not the best judges of what is ultimately good for us—God is.

THE FOURTH PRINCIPLE: WANTING WHAT WE WERE CREATED FOR

Principle 4. We should want only what we were created for.

Saint Augustine wrote, "You have created us for yourself, O Lord, and our hearts are restless until they rest in you."[1] He was right—we are restless, always looking for the thing in our lives that will make us happier, whether it be a person, a job, money, a place to live, an education, or a skill. John Lennon is said to have written, "Life is what happens when you're busy making other plans." Too much emphasis on what we think we want can derail us from ever really living. Instead of abolishing our desire, though, we should purify it. We should learn what we really need—what we were created for—and seek it wholeheartedly.

Exercise on Setting Our Priorities

It is very easy for us to lose sight of what is most important in our lives. Ignatius counsels us to recognize the ways we have lost sight of our priorities and to seek what is most important: the will of God, which is our eternal well-being. In this exercise, we pray that God might help us to recognize what is most valuable in our daily lives.

> *[Jesus said,] "Again, the kingdom of heaven is like a merchant in search of fine pearls, who, on finding one pearl of great value, went and sold all that he had and bought it." (Mt 13:45–46)*

Our eternal well-being is a pearl of great value; it is worth giving up everything for. Like athletes who give up all sorts of fun in order to train and who leave home and family in search of Olympic victory, we are encouraged to see all things in light of our ultimate goal. The apostle Paul wrote of his experience this way:

> *But whatever gain I had, I counted as loss for the sake of Christ. Indeed I count everything as loss because of the surpassing worth of knowing Christ Jesus my Lord. For his sake I have suffered the loss of all things, and count them as refuse, in order that I may gain Christ. (Phil 3:7–8)*

Return to meditating on the things in your life that make you rich. Do they make you happy? Do they help you to know God and to love people? If the answers are yes, then they are good. If the answers are no, then they aren't. As you continue your workouts, pay close attention to the things in your life, and measure them according to these two questions. Ask God to help you recognize the things that hinder you.

HOW TO APPROACH THE PRINCIPLES

If we are to build our lives on the proper foundation, we must seek to remove all the barriers in our lives that keep us from praising, reverencing, and serving God. It's a little bit like trying to get rich: before we can accumulate wealth, we've got to get ourselves out of debt. We must learn to recognize the spiritual deficits in our lives and work to remove them. An important aspect of this principle, then, is paying attention to these deficits, which in traditional theology are called "sin." Sin is any choice that diminishes us as human beings, preventing us from more fully living the end for which God created us. In the New Testament, the Greek word for *sin* literally means "missing the mark." It suggests that in trying to achieve our happiness, we sometimes have poor aim. A major part of the principles, then, is perfecting our aim. I like the image of archery: we may see the target at some distance but are unable to hit the bull's-eye. With practice, though, we can develop a keener sense of how to do this. The four workouts in part 2 are all about building upon this foundation so that we can perfect our aim of doing God's will in our lives.

In summary, let us recognize that the foundation represents our right relationship with God, which we then cultivate and learn from in the spiritual workouts. For many, embracing the foundation will take time and effort, for it will require a conversion, a change in worldview. The philosopher Aristotle wrote that growing in virtue is like unbending a stick. You can't make a bent stick straight all at once; you must constantly bend it back the other way, and over time, the stick will straighten out. Human beings are similar: you can't expect your worldview to change all at once. You can practice the exercises in this chapter and allow God to change you over time. In essence, the spiritual workouts are about letting God "bend" us to more perfectly accept the foundation so that we might achieve our freedom and happiness.

After you've spent some time on the foundation and are ready to work on deepening your understanding of God's work in your life, go on to part 2.

part

Workouts

IN THE NEXT FOUR CHAPTERS, WE WILL GO OVER THE FOUR WORKOUTS.
Remember that the rule of thumb in prayer is to do what works and
not to get caught up in trying to do everything perfectly. At certain
points, I will suggest specific exercises, but much of the work is up to
you. These workouts are meant to be guides that you can return to
later if necessary. There is no specific time frame attached to any of
the workouts. I suggest that you read the chapters straight through, in
order to see the terrain you are about to traverse. Then use the exercises that are given in summary form at the end of each chapter. The
exercises correspond to what is written earlier in the chapter. In the
exercises, apply the seven practices described in chapter 3.

It may be helpful to remember that originally each workout corre-
sponded to about a week of prayer. A different suggestion, for busy
people, is to read every few days, or even once a week, and to practice
one element of the workout on each occasion. Remember that if you
want to get the most out of these workouts, you should take them
slowly and deliberately. The objective is not to get through them but,
rather, to grow by doing them well.

first workout: understanding our perfection and imperfection

YOU'VE BEEN TO THE INTRODUCTORY MEETINGS WITH THE COACHING STAFF, learned about the training regimen, and prepared yourself for the season—now is the time to actually show up for the first day of practice! The only thing you know to anticipate is that it's impossible to anticipate what's going to happen. But you've psyched yourself up, and you're ready to begin. Let's see what the coach says.

The first workout is about coming to terms with the reality of who we are as human beings created in the image and likeness of God, though marred by sin. This workout, then, involves two stages: first, understanding ourselves as created by God; and second, understanding ourselves as people who sin.

Stage one is essentially a repetition of the first principle and foundation. Focus on how God has created you for God's own delight. There are three exercises at the end of this chapter that correspond to stage one—spend several days simply paying attention to the theme of God's delight in creating you.

Stage two involves an acknowledgment of our original goodness, which has become tarnished over time, like a silver plate that has lost its shine or a painting that has become covered in grime. We come before God, the artisan, to clean off God's original work of art. After you read this chapter, use the eight exercises of stage two, also listed at the end of the chapter. Take several days or weeks to spend time on these exercises.

MISSING THE MARK

There was a young man named Mike who was getting ready to head off to college, and as the end of the summer approached, he was really excited. He had lived with his father his whole life, and both he and his older brother, Will, were getting to the point of needing some space by themselves. Will had decided to help his father's business and so had not ever gone to college—but hoped to someday. Mike, though, was bold. Near the end of his senior year in high school, he went to his dad and basically said that he was leaving the following fall, having been accepted at the state university in the business program. His dad, proud but also a bit sad, said that of course he would help Mike out financially. In fact, as business for the past few years had been good, his dad really set him up nicely.

Mike found his freshman year a lot of fun—too much fun, actually, since he found the party scene to be more interesting than studying. His weekends began on Thursday evenings and usually ended after the Monday hangover wore off. About midway through the fall semester, Mike started to realize that he'd run out of cash before the end of the year, and he started to get a little concerned. He found an evening job off campus at a local grocery store, making minimum wage, and it bored him to death. His grades continued to suffer, even as he kept up his social life. By the end of the semester, he had failed out of school and had to move out of the residence hall. He was too embarrassed to go home to his father, so he stayed at a friend's off-campus apartment during the winter break, still working at the supermarket. He was miserable—all his friends had gone home, he was short on money, worked a boring job, and had squandered his chance at the university.

Eventually Mike decided he'd had enough and would go back home. He e-mailed his dad, saying he'd be on the next bus, but didn't say much more than that. When he arrived at the bus station, his dad was there, happy to see him after so many months. They headed home, and Mike saw his brother Will for the first time in a while, too. His dad remarked that they were having a New Year's Day bowl party and would invite some of the neighbors in the area whose kids were also students at the university—their football team was in the Orange Bowl this year, so it was a pretty big deal. Dad ordered lots of food and drinks for everyone and was happy to talk about how his son was a student at the university.

Mike had a great time at the party, even though he felt strange cheering on the team from the very university he'd just failed out of. He told his dad about the semester, fearing that he'd be angry, but his dad was really great about it. He didn't criticize Mike or make him feel bad but just told Mike he was glad to see him home again.

Will was pretty upset—here was a party all about Mike and his school, even though Mike had wasted his time there. He couldn't understand why his dad would let Mike off so easily. Will had never even had the chance to go to college, and he knew that Mike was more of a screwup than he was. He later told his dad about this. Dad just replied that it wasn't a reflection on Will but, rather, a chance to let Mike know that his dad still loved him.

This story is a version of the parable of the prodigal son (Lk 15). Many people have heard the parable, and for this reason often don't pay attention to what it's about. What I want to suggest is that it gives us a useful model for understanding "missing the mark" and therefore for understanding how our spiritual lives must involve recognizing how we must change.

The word *prodigal* means "excessive"—someone who spends too much. Some commentators have suggested that it is the father who is prodigal, for he spends too much on the son who didn't deserve it. In the parable, Jesus describes God this way, always seeking out the one who has gone away and chosen to return. God the Father is eager to welcome back those who have missed the mark and loves to celebrate our return lavishly. We have nothing to fear from deciding to make a change back to God.

This idea is so important because everyone finds himself or herself in a position like Mike's at some point in life. It is worth observing that Mike is not an evil person; at no point does he choose anything malicious. On the contrary, he is someone who just wants to have a good time; this is the way Jesus describes the prodigal son. I think everyone can identify with the experience of making choices that seem good and harmless, only to find out later that they are destructive, either to ourselves or to someone else. It is at these moments of our lives that the notion of "missing the mark" makes sense. We have tried to live right and make reasonable choices, but it seems that, at some point, we have gotten off track. We have missed the mark—we have missed the will of God.

The first workout is about understanding the first principle and foundation, and, at the same time, recognizing our tendencies toward sin. So as you come to have a better understanding of the foundation, ask God to help you recognize the choices in your life that contribute to your missing the mark. Ask for the understanding of the pain you have caused yourself and others, so that you might have better insight into avoiding bad choices in the future.

Sin is one of those topics that turn a lot of people off, so it may be helpful to take a moment to put Ignatius's ideas in some context.

Many are familiar with the graphic descriptions of sin and hell that we see, for example, in paintings or stories from centuries ago. I think of Michelangelo's fresco *The Last Judgment* on the wall of the Sistine Chapel, a towering imaginative depiction of the consequences of sin. In this picture, we see horrible demons literally grabbing and dragging unrepentant sinners into the fires of hell, while the sinners shriek in horrible agony. It's an intense and terrifying picture, consistent with the depictions of hell in famous works like Dante's *Inferno* or Milton's *Paradise Lost*. All of these works, which have had a great influence on Western ideas about sin and hell, were produced around the time Ignatius was writing and suggest something of the way people then thought about these topics. As a product of that era, Ignatius, too, was very influenced by these ideas, and so his sometimes graphic descriptions of sin can be frightening.

In the context of imaginative spiritual exercises, these depictions, which seem to us macabre and even distasteful, begin to make sense. If imagination helps us to more realistically confront things, then imagination about sin is no different. I think that these depictions were seen as attempts to help people confront the reality of their bad decisions, evil choices, thoughtless actions, spiteful words, careless attitudes. They put pictures to the outcomes of sin, making people really think about the consequences of what they did.

Today, in a culture of visual saturation (movies, TV, magazines, billboards, photographs, etc.), we need not imagine anything—it's all done for us. Our deepest emotions of fear, horror, sadness, and despair, as well as hope, love, joy, and happiness, are easily portrayed in various media. We don't need to think about these things, because our thoughts are already available in attractive ways for us to consume—prepackaged pathos.

One writer described how he would bring to his college class two types of writing. One was a poem, exquisitely penned by a well-known American poet of the twentieth century; the other, a short prose synopsis of the poem. He asked the class which writing they preferred, and inevitably they chose the second. The first one, they said, was too hard to understand. The writer, commenting on this

phenomenon, suggested simply that reading a poem took more thinking and that the students did not want to make the effort to understand the poem.

Often, I think, our attitudes toward sin are similar. We don't want
to confront the difficult problem of sin in our lives, as it manifests
itself in our relationships to God and others. We would rather comment on what is wrong with the world, because it's easier to respond
to a news story than to the problems in our souls. Seldom do we confront that there is something deeply flawed about ourselves. Ignatius's
contemporaries, I think, were much more willing to confront this
truth. They applied their imagination, as did Ignatius, to the reality
and consequences of sin, and created elaborate images for its destructive influence. Sin wrecks human beings, they said—it destroys the
very beauty that is God's creation.

Honesty demands that we confront the truth that sometimes our
choices have hurt people and that the failure to alter these choices
makes us lesser persons. As we progress through this second stage of the
first workout, Ignatius asks us to imagine the effects of our sins. This
consideration of how we have missed the mark is vitally important if
we are to make progress in our spiritual lives. The earlier analogy of a
coach critiquing an athlete's performance is helpful to keep in the back
of your mind as you go through this part of the workout: if we don't
understand how we are doing things wrong, we won't ever improve.

SIN

The story of Adam and Eve is an imaginative account of the original
sin of humanity: disobeying God. Consider what it suggests about the
way human beings fall into sin.

Now the serpent was more subtle than any other wild creature that
the LORD God had made. He said to the woman, "Did God say,
'You shall not eat of any tree of the garden'?" And the woman said
to the serpent, "We may eat of the fruit of the trees of the garden;

but God said, 'You shall not eat of the fruit of the tree which is in
the midst of the garden, neither shall you touch it, lest you die.'"
But the serpent said to the woman, "You will not die. For God
knows that when you eat of it your eyes will be opened, and you
will be like God, knowing good and evil." So when the woman saw
that the tree was good for food, and that it was a delight to the eyes,
and that the tree was to be desired to make one wise, she took of its
fruit and ate; and she also gave some to her husband, and he ate.
Then the eyes of both were opened, and they knew that they were
naked; and they sewed fig leaves together and made themselves
aprons. (Gn 3:1–7)

Note that in this story, the sin is not a deliberate malicious act. In some ways, it can be described as an immature choice—this is how it is regarded by some Jewish rabbinic readings. One can imagine a young child being deceived by an older brother or sister in a similar way. The older sibling says, "Sure you can eat a cookie now! Mom won't mind!" And the younger sibling believes it because he or she wants to. This idea of sin being a deliberate choice to believe what we want to believe is very suggestive. In what ways have you made choices in your life based on something you wanted to believe? What consequences exist because of these choices?

The story moves us to consider one of the fundamental experiences of alienation that all human beings experience: that involving our sexuality. The consequence of the characters' sin, it notes, is shame about their nakedness. Sin, it seems, makes them self-conscious; and whereas before they were naively content with being naked, now it makes them uncomfortable. This observation suggests that the very experience of alienation between man and woman is a consequence of sin. This is not difficult to connect to ordinary experience: men and women have, over history, been alienated, and the most obvious consequence of this alienation has been the suppression of women's freedom. Today this is still the case in many ways. Our attitudes toward sexuality have led, for example, to advertisers' glorification of unrealistic images of women's bodies; to the expectation that women's sex drives must behave like men's; to the widespread acceptance of popular pornography; and to the self-mutilation practiced, disturbingly, among many adolescent girls. We live in an age and a society that has rejected older norms of sexuality, and we are still in the process of developing new ones. Without these norms, many people are hurt. We must consider how, even without intending it, our own attitudes have led to people getting hurt.

Another provocative element in the story is the theme of wanting to be like God. One theologian has suggested that the key to the spiritual life is understanding two things: that only God is God and that we human beings are God's creatures. It seems that in many of our choices, we express our desire to be our own gods; we want the power to create our lives as we wish, not wanting to admit our dependence on God. Many young people, especially, feel invincible—we want to determine the course of our own lives, and because of the world we live in today, we have much greater freedom than so many others have enjoyed. It is easy to fall into the trap of thinking we are self-reliant and that we do not need God: with so many resources at our disposal, it seems easy to feed our spiritual hunger. Eventually, though, it becomes clear that no one is capable of filling every desire of the heart. We must consider the role of God in our lives. Is God at the center or somewhere on the periphery? In what ways have you taken God's role in your life? In what ways do you need God? What are the most profound desires of your heart?

DESTROYING OUR RELATIONSHIP WITH GOD

Consider the story of David and Bathsheba (2 Sm 11–12). King David had an affair with the wife of one of his subjects and then sent the husband off to the front line of the war so he would be killed. It was a deliberate, malicious sin on the part of the king that God himself had chosen for the land of Israel. God sent the prophet Nathan to confront David with the gravity of his sin; and when David realized what he had done, he repented. Psalm 51 is attributed to David when he realized what he had done:

Have mercy on me, God, in your goodness;
  in your abundant compassion blot out my offense.
Wash away all my guilt;
  from my sin cleanse me.
For I know my offense;
  my sin is always before me.
Against you alone have I sinned;
  I have done such evil in your sight
That you are just in your sentence,
  blameless when you condemn.
True, I was born guilty,
  a sinner, even as my mother conceived me.
Still, you insist on sincerity of heart;
  in my inmost being teach me wisdom.
Cleanse me with hyssop, that I may be pure;
  wash me, make me whiter than snow.
Let me hear sounds of joy and gladness;
  let the bones you have crushed rejoice.

Turn away your face from my sins;
  blot out all my guilt.
A clean heart create for me, God;
  renew in me a steadfast spirit.
Do not drive me from your presence,
  nor take from me your holy spirit. (Ps 51:3–13 NAB)

This prayer, called the *Miserere* in Latin, has been used in liturgical settings for the purpose of asking God's forgiveness for human sins. Everyone can identify with the sentiment of the song, for it arises out of the experience of guilt. Turning to God under this circumstance can be frightening; it is never easy to acknowledge doing something wrong and facing God in our shame. For this reason, many people avoid ever acknowledging guilt. They respond in anger to anyone who might point out their faults, and thus they never give themselves the opportunity to grow as people.

In this first workout, it is vitally important to acknowledge and name our sins. This is not simply a morbid exercise designed to make us feel bad about ourselves; it is, rather, an honest attempt to identify those parts of our lives that need improvement. No one can grow in any way, be it as an athlete or intellectually or spiritually, unless he or she becomes aware of mistakes and wrongdoings. So the purpose here is to become more deeply aware of our guilt and the negative effect it has on our relationship to God and on our ability to become good people. In this segment of the workout, then, our prayer (paradoxically) is that we might feel the pain of our sins. This is not an end in itself but, rather, a means to the greater end of resolving to avoid our sins in the future. If we wish to avoid mistakes, we must begin with the resolve that they are truly serious, and this resolve must be on both an intellectual and an emotional level. In short, we want to develop a repugnance for sin and a love for doing the will of God. Our prayer must reflect the attitude of the psalmist who wrote, "In my heart I treasure your promise, / that I may not sin against you," and "How I love your teaching, LORD! / I study it all day long." (Ps 119:11, 97 NAB). We must learn to hate our own sin and love God alone.

GUILT AND MERCY

Imagine speaking directly with Jesus on the cross. As you do this, consider these lines from Scripture:

God shows his love for us in that while we were yet sinners Christ died for us. (Rom 5:8)

Thus, sinning against your brethren and wounding their conscience when it is weak, you sin against Christ. (1 Cor 8:12)

He himself bore our sins in his body on the tree, that we might die to sin and live to righteousness. By his wounds you have been healed. (1 Pt 2:24)

In this the love of God was made manifest among us, that God sent his only Son into the world, so that we might live through him. In this is love, not that we loved God but that he loved us and sent his Son to be the expiation for our sins. (1 Jn 4:9–10)

Grace to you and peace from God the Father and our Lord Jesus Christ, who gave himself for our sins to deliver us from the present evil age, according to the will of our God and Father. (Gal 1:3–4)

As you imagine the scene of Jesus on the cross, again try to apply all your senses. What do you see? What do you hear around you? What are the smells and tastes in your mouth? What does the air feel like? Now, as you look at Jesus, what do you say? Consider how you feel about these questions:

What have I done for Christ?
What am I doing for Christ?
What will I do for Christ?

Speak whatever is on your mind and later think about what these words tell you about yourself.

This imaginative conversation with Jesus crucified is an important part of the first workout, for in it we are confronting the reality of who we are before God. It is the opportunity to honestly assess our weaknesses, to come to greater awareness of the parts of our lives that we must resolve to change if we are to grow spiritually. But it is also a chance to confront Jesus at his weakest moment, when (according to

Matthew and Mark) he cries out, "My God, my God! Why have you abandoned me?"

It is easy for us, living two millennia after the time of Jesus, to see him as an abstract figure, distant and removed from our everyday experience. To really imagine Jesus as a man suffering torture and death can be disturbing. But this experience is meant to provoke us to think of sin in very concrete terms: what I do wrong is what led this man to his death. I admit that I find this kind of meditation very difficult. Generally speaking, our culture tends to avoid some of the more messy parts of human life; we have developed particularly unhealthy attitudes toward violence and death, especially. And so we who are part of this culture aren't accustomed to thinking about suffering very much. In contrast, people of different times and places in Christian history were more interested in the theme of Christ's suffering. This attitude shows up, for example, in some paintings and sculptures that show Christ's wounds with graphic detail. At the college where I teach, there is one such example. It is a statue of Christ all broken and bloodied; it is so awful to look at that the statue is adorned with a cape around all but the figure's head. Most people I know find it rather repulsive; it provokes a reaction of disgust, contrary to what many think spirituality ought to be about.

In the context of this workout, though, it is easier to see why images like the statue have been part of the Christian landscape for centuries. Like the images of hell I described earlier, this image of a bloodied Christ helps the person to imagine what Jesus really went through because he loved God. It is easy to sometimes gloss over the fact that this man was tortured because of his faithfulness to the will of God; we tend to more often think of the risen Christ as someone who has a blissful face and issues peace to everyone free of charge.

One sad truth of human existence, though, is that violence makes people confront reality. This became all too clear to me as I have reflected on the events of September 11, 2001. The violence that so many people saw that day made them honestly confront both the dark side of human existence and the human potential for heroism and self-sacrifice. And in this, the cross is similar: it forces us to confront both the evil that human beings perpetrate and the nobility of giving one's life out of selfless love. We must see Jesus as one who, not unlike the rescuers killed in the World Trade Center, suffered because of his choice to love.

PERSPECTIVE ON WHO WE ARE

This meditation naturally leads into the next important theme: namely, that we ourselves have contributed to the very evil that led to Jesus' death. We too are sinners; we too have exacerbated the alienation of human beings from God that Jesus sought to reconcile. Thus, in this prayer, we ask God for an awareness of the ways that we have helped cause this rift. We pray for a kind of catharsis, a state of sincere sorrow for all the evil we have done. And so Ignatius counsels that we imagine a courtroom proceeding, during which the prosecutor gives a record of all our sins. As we listen to the prosecutor reading off the list of things we have done wrong throughout our lives, we are to consider what we truly deserve. With these choices, we have slowly tarnished the original beauty of God's good creation of us. We have taken a work of art and smeared graffiti all over it so that it is no longer beautiful. We have made ourselves less than what we were intended to be.

In light of this meditation, we can begin to get a different perspective on who we are. Consider the following questions:

- Who am I compared to all the other people in the world? I am one small person in a world of billions of people.
- Who am I compared to all the good men and women who have gone before me: my ancestors, whose hope was that their descendants, like me, might live in happiness; the heroes and heroines who fought in many ways to secure my freedom, my right to autonomy; the holy people who died to pass on the faith that I have received as a gift?

- Who am I in the context of the whole of creation? One person on one small planet in one small solar system on the outskirts of one of millions of galaxies. I am less than a speck of dust; I barely merit being identified as a single atom in a speck of dust.
- Who am I compared to God? One small atom on one speck of dust in the midst of the whole of creation that God made. What can I be apart from God? Why has God chosen to care for me?

We live our lives behind the camera of our own consciousness, recording our experiences from this limited perspective. As the documentary that is our life unfolds, we encounter different people and things coming into the foreground and dropping into the background. Some retain importance for a time; but later the scene changes, and we are somewhere different. Experiences change, but our perspective remains the same: we are in charge of the production; we are the center of the world. This exercise reminds us that ours is not the only show, though; in fact, it isn't even prime-time material. To us, our lives are the most important thing, but what is this to eternity? Consider what Job says to God after hearing God's diatribe against Job's arrogance:

> *I know that you can do all things,*
>   *and that no purpose of yours can be hindered.*
> *I have dealt with great things that I do not understand;*
>   *things too wonderful for me, which I cannot know.*
> *I had heard of you by word of mouth,*
>   *but now my eye has seen you.*
> *Therefore I disown what I have said,*
>   *and repent in dust and ashes. (Jb 42:2–6 NAB)*

We must come to understand our lives as gifts of God at every moment. With each breath we take, God renews the gift. Our very lives are testaments to the mercy of God; for while we have constantly sinned, God continues to give us life. Consider God's words from the book of Micah:

"O my people, what have I done to you, / or how have I wearied you? Answer me!" (6:3 NAB). God's creation is gift upon gift upon gift; the world is charged with God's grandeur, and yet we still choose to sin. Let this meditation close, then, with thankfulness to God and the resolution to become a new creation, a renewed creature whose original beauty testifies to the glory of the creator. "Wash me, and I shall be whiter than snow" (Ps 51:7).

HELL

Think about what hell means. Avoid simply rehearsing the images from movies or TV, especially the kind of horror-movie demons that portray hell almost as somewhere interesting to visit for the thrill of it. Instead, consider what a self-chosen absence from the love of God would be like. Remember that in many places Jesus speaks of hell as the consequence of a life badly lived; and while the images he uses were those accessible to a first-century imagination and might be limiting, it is still possible to understand something of what he is exhorting people to choose: namely, the love of God over sin.

I say to you that every one who is angry with his brother shall be liable to judgment; whoever insults his brother shall be liable to the council, and whoever says, "You fool!" shall be liable to the hell of fire. (Mt 5:22)

Just as the weeds are gathered and burned with fire, so will it be at the close of the age. The Son of man will send his angels, and they will gather out of his kingdom all causes of sin and all evildoers, and throw them into the furnace of fire; there men will weep and gnash their teeth. (Mt 13:40–42)

Then [the king] will say to those on his left, "Depart from me, you accursed, into the eternal fire prepared for the devil and his angels. For I was hungry and you gave me no food, I was thirsty and you gave me no drink, a stranger and you gave me no welcome, naked and you gave me no clothing, ill and in prison, and you did not care for me." Then they will answer and say, "Lord, when did we see you hungry or thirsty or a stranger or naked or ill or in prison, and not minister to your needs?" He will answer them, "Amen, I say to you, what you did not do for one of these least ones, you did not do for me." And these will go off to eternal punishment, but the righteous to eternal life. (Mt 25:41–46 NAB)

Jesus tells us that hell is real; and while we can never know who has chosen it, still this image reminds us that our life choices have ultimate consequences. These consequences are not arbitrary but, rather, due to our failure to love God by loving others. As you close this prayer, then, ask God to give you greater compassion so that you may show mercy to other people the way that God has shown mercy to you.

SUMMARY OF THE FIRST WORKOUT

As a man trained in the military, Ignatius was no doubt influenced by the model of training soldiers for war. Like boot camp, the first stage carries a theme of breaking down our resistance. If we are to allow God to remake us in our original beauty, we must undergo a difficult process of breakdown. The biblical image of a gold refiner may be helpful here: gold is purified by subjecting it to intense heat, thus burning away any imperfections. God too removes our imperfections, but this is never easy. We must confront the darker parts of ourselves if we want God to heal them.

This workout is about coming to a strong, emotional sense of dependence on God, recognizing that we alone are incapable of reforming our lives without God. Once we begin to understand how much we need God for our happiness, we are ready to move on to the second workout.

EXERCISES IN THE FIRST WORKOUT

Remember the seven practices: gaining interior peace; practicing the presence of God; making a preparatory prayer; using your imagination; making your requests known; engaging in a closing conversation with God; and repeating what works for you. Try to apply them to the exercises below.

Stage One

1. Meditating on Why You Were Created

Create an imaginative scene in your mind wherein God is creating you, "knitting you in your mother's womb," to use the language of Psalm 139. What is God creating you for? What does God particularly enjoy about this creation? What tasks has God put before you in life? Imagine talking with God about why you were created. What does God say?

2. Turning Your Liabilities into Strengths

Consider one element in your life that many would consider a liability, as in the case of the blind man:

> *As he passed by, he saw a man blind from his birth. And his disciples asked him, "Rabbi, who sinned, this man or his parents, that he was born blind?" Jesus answered, "It was not that this man sinned, or his parents, but that the works of God might be made manifest in him." (Jn 9:1–3)*

Ask God why you were created this way. How might "the works of God be made manifest" in you?

3. Discovering the Riches in Your Life

Recall the story of the rich man and Lazarus. Pay attention to the things that make you rich. Ask whether they also help you to praise, reverence, and serve God.

Stage Two

1. Learning from the Story of the Prodigal Son

Read the story of the prodigal son (Lk 15:11–32). Imagine yourself in the place of each of the characters: the prodigal son, the prodigal father, the older son. What do you learn about yourself as each of these characters? What do you learn about God?

2. Recognizing Where You've Missed the Mark

Ask God to help you recognize your sins as you pray over the story of Adam and Eve. In what ways have you disobeyed God? In what ways have you missed the mark?

3. Confronting Your Sin

Read the story of Nathan confronting David with his sin (2 Sm 11–12) and David's response (Ps 51). Put yourself in the place of David. Notice that David inadvertently judges himself. As you imagine the scene, try to focus on the feeling of facing up to your sin. What do you really deserve?

4. Speaking to Jesus on the Cross

Read one of the crucifixion accounts of Jesus in the Gospels. Speak to Jesus on the cross, and pay attention to your emotions as you apply your senses to the scene.

5. Facing Up to Your Sin before God

Imagine the courtroom scene, in which all your sins are read out before God. Try to remember details about your sins: what led you to your choices and what the consequences were (or are). Focus on what it feels like to face up to this sin before God.

6. Gaining Perspective on Who You Are

Do the meditation on who we are compared to the rest of creation, as described earlier in this chapter.

7. Understanding the Meaning of Hell

Create an image of hell. Is it fire? Eternity with someone you hate? Loss of something you love?

8. Making Your Confession

Ignatius suggests that a person make a confession at the end of the first workout. For some, this suggestion will mean seeking the sacrament of reconciliation. The sacrament of reconciliation is not, primarily, about telling someone your secrets. Like all the sacraments, it is based in the recognition that there is always some human action or context within which God self-reveals. In this case, the human action is "getting something off our chest" or simply the action of giving words to something we've done wrong. (Twelve-step programs recognize this same basic need that people have—to tell someone when they've done something wrong.) It is about naming our sins so that we can ask God for forgiveness. In the context of the sacramental life of the church, reconciliation is about joining with all the other sinners in asking God to perfect us as individuals and as a community.

chapter 6

second workout:
following the leader

I REMEMBER THE IMPATIENCE I FELT THE VERY FIRST TIME I GOT INTO A
boat, anticipating the fun of racing across the water. The boat was
a huge, floating barge used to train novices, about as apt for racing as
a tractor trailer in the Indianapolis 500. We spent several practices in
this barge, just learning basic points about our strokes, and it wasn't
until later that we were even allowed into a racing shell. When that
finally happened, I thought to myself, The fun is really about to start!
But I was wrong. Even in the shell, we rowed in pairs, which is hard
work when there are eight people to carry along. It took another several practices before all eight people rowed together. And we realized

why it took so long! As soon as we started, the boat flipped from side to side, water splashed everywhere, and it felt really uncomfortable. Evidently rowing an eight was not as easy as it looked.

This lesson in patience was hard. So many times in our lives, we confront the difference between our expectations and reality, and we can be disappointed. Sometimes we have to abandon our expectations altogether; other times, we must be prepared at least to modify them. So it is with prayer. The purpose of the first workout is to practice attentiveness to God's will in our lives; and for many people, this workout can be very difficult. It can take a long time to break old habits and to look at the world in a new way. But once we do, we are more ready to learn new ways of responding to God.

The second workout builds on the foundation of the first, in that it relies on the principle of seeking God in all things. In this workout, the primary aim is discerning the specific ways God is calling us to live—as single or married or vowed religious; as student, homemaker, businessperson, medical worker, public servant, artist, educator, or anything else. The key word is *vocation,* a term that comes from the Latin word meaning "to call." Once, this term applied strictly to the priesthood or religious life, but today many use it to refer to any of the ways that God calls us to use our gifts and talents for God's greater glory. What makes our daily life a vocation is our willingness to use it as a way of praising God, regardless of how mundane or boring it may currently seem to us.

St. Ignatius had to make a decision in his own life about the path he chose to take: following his own desire for military glory or following the humble ways of Jesus Christ. This personal decision became an important theme in the *Spiritual Exercises.* The second workout focuses on this theme and uses the image of the king so that we might confront the question of whom we choose to follow. Today, of course, there no longer exist knights and kings, but the image of these characters is strong enough that we can understand the kind of point Ignatius was making.

To prepare for the second workout, Ignatius asks that we picture a king whom God chooses and who speaks to all his people in preparation for war. The image makes me think about the movies *Braveheart,* *Gladiator,* or *Henry V.* All of these movies have scenes in which the leader prepares his troops for battle, rousing their hearts and minds for the coming fight. He asks the soldiers to join him in vanquishing the foe; and his honor and heroism move all to pledge their lives to his service. As a former soldier, Ignatius himself was intimately familiar with this kind of image. He recognized that the king on the battlefield represents in his very person the ideals for which soldiers are prepared to give their lives.

Ignatius asks us to consider whom we are to follow with the same sobriety as the soldier preparing for battle. This imaginative exercise is to help us remember the seriousness of our life decisions, in order that we may come to greater clarity about the kinds of lives we choose to lead. Today, perhaps, imagining a king is too distant, too Hollywood for us to make our own. But we can nevertheless benefit from considering who our models, heroes, and leaders are.

To begin, think of a person whom you greatly admire the kind of person who represents to you the model of how God asks human beings to live and whom you would immediately follow if he or she asked you. What is important to imagine is your own emotional response to this person: complete willingness, along with excitement at being chosen, perhaps fear at the task, and even some indecision about whether the person made a mistake in choosing you. Imagine yourself completely taken by this request, free from whatever cynicism or doubt that may be part of your past experiences. Focus on the feeling of having a purpose in life, to carry out the task that this hero or heroine entrusts to you alone.

This feeling of having a life purpose is the subject of the second workout. The basic idea is that if a person we admire can entrust us with a responsibility that gives our lives meaning, then surely Christ can do this to an even greater extent.

Imagine that Christ came to you one day and said, "I need you, and you are the only person in the whole world who can do this. Will you help me?" Who could refuse? Who wouldn't want to be an agent sent by Christ himself? But then imagine that Christ said, "I need you to be a friend to the old woman who lives next door to you." What would you do? There is a certain glamour in having a life purpose, imagining that everything one does in life is oriented toward some great ideal. But it's very different if one's life purpose is to carry out a very mundane task. It is much easier to imagine following Christ as a knight sent on brave errands than as an ordinary person befriending a widow. For most of us, Christ's call will look much more like the second option. It will not be glamorous or exciting; in fact, much of the time it might be pretty ordinary. But if we are following Christ, then even the ordinary becomes part of the fabric of a holy life.

There is no escape from the ordinary. No matter who we are, no matter what we do, there are going to be parts of our lives that are repetitious and boring. What makes these periods tolerable is the knowledge that they contribute to something greater. In my own experience is a time when this became clear. One Saturday, my team-mates and I were preparing to travel to a race in a distant city. This was a tedious process: we had to dismantle the boats, load them up for travel, secure them, collect all the foot stretchers and seats and oars, on and on. It took a long time to accomplish all this work, and on this particular day, we had to do it in the rain. It was miserable. Eventually someone remarked, "Do you realize that we train for fif-teen hours a week, just to do a six-minute race?" The ratio was stag-gering—I had never thought about it. Soon I could see that everyone there, like me, was doing some math in his head to figure out the total amount of work we did every season compared to how much time we actually did what we loved: racing. The numbers were absolutely ridiculous! At that moment, it hardly seemed possible that we tolerated so much work. And yet we were back at it the next week!

The point, of course, is that not all training is work; it can be very enjoyable. In our daily lives, too, there is a great deal of work—we all have those things that have to get done just so that we can function. But sometimes even the mundane can be transformed: the trip to the grocery store can be a time to chat; doing the laundry can be an occa-sion to read an interesting article; driving to pick up the kids can be a chance to enjoy some fresh air. More important, though, what makes us able to do these chores again and again is the knowledge that they serve a greater good in our lives.

In this second workout, we take a look at how our lives serve Christ, even in the ordinary things. We also have the chance to ask the question, "Do I need to make a change in my life in order to serve Christ more fully?" We begin by meditating on Christ's experience of living a human life, in order to learn how to follow his example. What kind of a king, or leader, is Christ? And how does he call us to follow him? As in the first workout, it is good to take your time. There are many scenes from the Gospels in this workout, any of which can be the subject of a day's prayer. Read the chapter, then do the exercises listed at the end of the chapter, using the seven practices.

CHRIST THE KING

The Scope of the Kingdom

We begin by considering the scope of the kingdom, imagining that we are with God the Father, Son, and Holy Spirit during the creation of the world. Imagine that you can see God actually forming all that is around us: you are outside of history and so can see the way God works through the forces of nature to bring about the origin of humankind. You see the animals and the earliest hominids, you witness the development of human intelligence, you see the formation of ancient clans and eventually cities. But you also see that in this beautiful creation, something has gone wrong—people are killing each other and acting with hatred toward those around them. People are spread out over the earth, suffering and asking God for help. God sends the Son to redeem this creation. You focus your attention on a city, Jerusalem. To the north of that city is a town called Nazareth. From your "God's eye" view, you witness an extraordinary moment: a teenager is going about her daily chores when she is surprised by the visit of a stranger named Gabriel. This is the story of the annunciation of Jesus' birth.

In the beginning God created the heavens and the earth. The earth was without form and void, and darkness was upon the face of the deep; and the Spirit of God was moving over the face of the waters. And God said, "Let there be light"; and there was light. And God saw that the light was good; and God separated the light from the darkness. (Gn 1:1–4)

In the beginning was the Word, and the Word was with God, and the Word was God. He was in the beginning with God; all things were made through him, and without him was not anything made that was made. In him was life, and the life was the light of men. The light shines in the darkness, and the darkness has not overcome it. (Jn 1:1–5)

In the sixth month the angel Gabriel was sent from God to a city of Galilee named Nazareth, to a virgin betrothed to a man whose name was Joseph, of the house of David; and the virgin's name was Mary. And he came to her and said, "Hail, O favored one, the Lord is with you!" But she was greatly troubled at the saying, and considered in her mind what sort of greeting this might be. And the angel said to her, "Do not be afraid, Mary, for you have found favor with God. And behold, you will conceive in your womb and bear a son, and you shall call his name Jesus." (Lk 1:26–31)

The Birth of Jesus

Next, we consider the stories around Jesus' birth: how Mary and Joseph had to travel south to Bethlehem, in response to the orders of the governor, who wanted to conduct a census. Let us travel with this family.

And Joseph also went up from Galilee, from the city of Nazareth, to Judea, to the city of David, which is called Bethlehem, because he was of the house and lineage of David, to be enrolled with Mary,

his betrothed, who was with child. And while they were there, the
time came for her to be delivered. And she gave birth to her first-
born son and wrapped him in swaddling cloths, and laid him in a
manger, because there was no place for them in the inn. (Lk 2:4–7)

On this journey of several days, we consider all that is around us: the
hot, dry air; the dust; the smell of the donkey that Mary is riding;
the weariness of our feet and the chafe of our sandals; our hunger
and thirst; the rugged terrain and the worn road we travel. Eventually
we experience the frustration of having no place at the inn and having to find somewhere clean and dry. Mary, at this point, is ready to
tear Joseph's hair out but says nothing because she's still young and
rather shy. Joseph wants to throttle the governor for this stupid census rule because it's made him have to uproot himself from his job to
bring his new family back to where he was born—and he left it in
the first place because it was awful living there. So there's a good deal
of tension in the air, made worse by the fact that Mary is already
showing signs of being ready to deliver. You wait with Mary as
Joseph searches out some old childhood acquaintances to request
some help in finding a place to stay. What do you talk about? How
do you divert her mind from all these worries? You can see that as a
first-time mom, she's a little scared at the prospect of having to give
birth, and so you try to help her avoid dwelling on that.

Eventually Joseph returns with news of a place to stay: it's pretty
sparse. In fact, it's little more than a roof, where some animals
sleep. Mary just wants to sleep, so you all go there and just lie
down in the hay. In the middle of the night, Mary begins her labor,
and after many hours, Jesus is born. Contemplate the scene: What
are Joseph and Mary doing? What does it feel like to be there? How
do you react when you first see the baby? Focus your attention now
on the theme of Christ's kingship and the paradox of seeing him
born in such meager conditions. Why was the Son of God born
under these conditions rather than in a palace? Why did he choose
this couple to be his (adoptive) parents? Why this obscure place,
with so little fanfare?

The Childhood and Youth of Jesus

We then imagine scenes of Jesus' childhood and youth: the presentation in the temple and the flight into Egypt, stories that illustrate how Mary and Joseph sought to listen to the voice of God.

> *When the days were completed for their purification according to the law of Moses, they took him up to Jerusalem to present him to the Lord, just as it is written in the law of the Lord, "Every male that opens the womb shall be consecrated to the Lord," and to offer the sacrifice of "a pair of turtledoves or two young pigeons," in accordance with the dictate in the law of the Lord.*
>
> *Now there was a man in Jerusalem whose name was Simeon. This man was righteous and devout, awaiting the consolation of Israel, and the holy Spirit was upon him. It had been revealed to him by the holy Spirit that he should not see death before he had seen the Messiah of the Lord. He came in the Spirit into the temple; and when the parents brought in the child Jesus to perform the custom of the law in regard to him, he took him into his arms and blessed God, saying:*

> *"Now, Master, you may let your servant go*
> *   in peace, according to your word,*
> *for my eyes have seen your salvation,*
> *   which you prepared in sight of all the peoples,*
> *a light for revelation to the Gentiles,*
> *   and glory for your people Israel." (Lk 2:22–32 NAB)*

> *The angel of the Lord appeared to Joseph in a dream and said, "Rise, take the child and his mother, flee to Egypt, and stay there until I tell you. Herod is going to search for the child to destroy him." Joseph rose and took the child and his mother by night and departed for Egypt. (Mt 2:13–14 NAB)*

Jesus Teaching in the Synagogue

The next scene is Jesus as a young man, when he taught in the synagogue.

> *Now his parents went to Jerusalem every year at the feast of the Passover. And when he was twelve years old, they went up according to custom; and when the feast was ended, as they were returning, the boy Jesus stayed behind in Jerusalem. His parents did not know it, but supposing him to be in the company they went a day's journey, and they sought him among their kinsfolk and acquaintances; and when they did not find him, they returned to Jerusalem, seeking him. After three days they found him in the temple, sitting among the teachers, listening to them and asking them questions; and all who heard him were amazed at his understanding and his answers. And when they saw him they were astonished; and his mother said to him, "Son, why have you treated us so? Behold, your father and I have been looking for you anxiously." And he said to them, "How is it that you sought me? Did you not know that I must be in my Father's house?" (Lk 2:41–49)*

Imagine this twelve year old under these circumstances. Put yourself into the story: first as one of the men listening to the boy Jesus; then as Mary or Joseph upon learning that your son is missing ("I thought he was with *you!* Oh, great!"). Finally, imagine yourself in Jesus' place. What has motivated you to stay behind in the temple? Why do you feel so drawn to talk with others who are studying the Holy Scriptures? How do you feel about staying in your "Father's house"? Consider the words of Psalm 27:

> *One thing I ask of the LORD;*
>   *this I seek:*
> *To dwell in the LORD's house*
>   *all the days of my life,*

> *To gaze on the* LORD's *beauty,*
> *to visit his temple. (Ps 27:4 NAB)*

It is worth contemplating this last image because it is so different from what we normally consider. For many, the last place they would want to live is inside a church or temple! But this image of dwelling "in the house of the Lord" is a common theme, especially throughout the Old Testament. It suggests being under the protection and care of God at all times, sheltered from evil and suffering, and embracing what is good and holy at all times. It is a state of perfect freedom, in which one has everything one needs and wants without fear of losing it. Imagine, then, what "the house of the Lord" would mean to you: What do you seek in your life, such that in possessing it, you would have all you need? What, in short, would bring you the greatest fulfillment as a human being?

Discerning the answer to this question moves us closer to what *vocation* means. A person's vocation is that state of life to which God calls him or her. It is the place where one's talents, energies, attractions, hopes, and aspirations lead, and so it can be described as the place in life where a person "fits." In the story, Jesus "fits" among the men in the temple, those who pore over the sacred Torah to understand God's law for human living. It is important to recognize several points about this story, to help us understand further what vocation is all about.

First, note that although his parents brought him there, Jesus discovers his love of this place by himself. There is a spontaneity in learning one's vocation—it comes upon us as a love of what we are doing. But we must be prepared to watch for it always! Jesus' parents brought him many places, no doubt, but there was something about this particular place that attracted him. It's a good thing he wasn't too distracted by playing on his new Game Boy while listening to all the latest tracks he downloaded on his MP3 player!

Second, it seems that Jesus loses all track of time while in the temple. His parents left much earlier—a whole day passes! Jesus is so caught up in what he is doing that every other priority in his life takes a back seat. I imagine Jesus' situation here as something like some of the late-night talks I've had with close friends. Time blows by because I'm so much in the moment and don't give a thought to anything else.

Third, the scene in the story is clearly a foreshadowing of what is to become Jesus' adult life. Even at twelve, Luke tells us, Jesus is committed to discerning the will of the Father, and so it is no surprise that preaching about the kingdom of God becomes Jesus' purpose later in life. For us, this suggests that there might be hints throughout our lives of what God created us to do. What were you good at when you were young? What did you most enjoy? Did adults ever make comments to you or your parents about how good you were at something? As you look back at your life today, what strikes you as being a foreshadowing of who you are now?

Fourth, as we consider this story in the light of the rest of the Gospel, an important theme emerges. Jesus is committed to his vocation, of which this story in the temple is a hint. Jesus' vocation unfolds naturally; he doesn't have to force it by working extraordinarily hard, only to be disappointed later. On the flip side, though, this vocation does not come easily. Jesus undergoes temptation, suffers rejection and misunderstanding, withstands accusations, and even dies a martyr's death for what he believes. He sometimes questions what he is doing, as in the Garden of Gethsemane before his crucifixion, but he never ultimately wavers from the conviction that this is what his life is about. He is so committed to what the Father calls him to do that nothing stands in his way of accomplishing it.

Fifth, then, let us recognize, soberly, that in many ways, Jesus failed in his vocation. It is clear that he longed to bring about a greater understanding of God's will in people's lives, but so many seemed to misunderstand him. There are points where he vents his frustration— for example, in the scene when he lashes out at the moneylenders in the temple precincts (Mk 11:15–18). Here is a man who desires much and is disappointed by what he is able to see. Even his disciples, whom he hopes better understand what he is doing with his life, seem to miss what Jesus is doing: "how long will I be with you and endure you?" he says at one point (Lk 9:41 NAB). Before his death, we see a man who likely wondered whether he was a failure.

This last point suggests that our own harsh judgments of ourselves may be limited and that in living out our vocations, we can only trust that God's call to us is greater than we can fully understand. Can we really know how we have made a difference? Could the Jesus who showed his own terror at an impending death (Lk 22:41–44) have understood how he would change the world? The bottom line is that Jesus pursued God's calling not primarily in order to accomplish a specific goal but, rather, because it was simply what he had to do to live. For Jesus, there was no other way to live than to preach the kingdom of God.

Practicing the art of self-understanding is the key to the discernment of vocation. Our vocation is that to which we are called because of our unique talents. In living out our vocation, we express the very reason for which God created us, and in doing so, we give glory to God even before we open our mouths to speak forth prayer.

YOUR VOCATION

The second workout is an apt time for us to raise specific questions about vocation. In meditating on the life of Jesus, we can consider him as our role model of obedience to the will of God. In this part of our workout, though, we have to take some initiative if we are to learn more clearly the answer to the question, "What does God want from *me?*"

Making a Life Decision

There are two kinds of choices we face at different periods of our lives. The first is the choice of what kind of life to live; the second is how to improve the life we already have. Examples of the first kind happen often during young adulthood: whether to go to college,

whether to take a certain job or enter religious life, whether to continue a serious relationship or get married, whether to have children,
and so on. These decisions can be difficult because we are always
faced with uncertainty about what the future holds. If you are in a
position to make this kind of decision, bring it specifically into your
prayer life. Here are some ideas about how to do this:

- First, reflect on the first principle and foundation: whatever
  you choose, it should help you to praise God and lead you to
  your ultimate well-being.
- Consider whether your proposed decision serves others or
  whether it serves only yourself. Your decision should enable
  you to love God more because it enables you to love other
  people more.
- Consider whether the decision is permanent or temporary.
  For example, if it is marriage or religious life, these involve
  permanent vows. If the decision is temporary, like doing volunteer work for a year or two, it requires a different kind of
  commitment.
- In the case of a decision that is already made, but without
  enough preparation, the issue is how to live according to
  God's will in spite of earlier mistakes. One example is unexpected parenthood: even if you did not plan to become a parent, you can still bring into prayer your desire to do God's
  will. Perhaps that means learning to be a single parent or loving the child into an adoptive family.
- Pay attention to your emotions and your reasoning. Be careful to distinguish what kind of emotions you are feeling!
  There is a difference between the happiness one feels, for
  example, when winning a bet and the happiness one feels
  when told "thank you" by someone you've helped. Allow your
  reasoning to help you understand which kind of emotion is
  more attuned to the whisper of God.
- Imagine someone is writing the story of your life. What
  do you want this chapter to be about? Similarly, imagine

speaking to God after you have died. What would God say
about your decision?

- Imagine yourself much older, counseling the you of today.
What do you think the older you would say to the younger
you?
- Judge whether the proposed decision will help you live with
greater faith, hope, and love.

The second kind of life decision faces us when we are already estab-
lished in a way of life but raise questions about whether we are doing
it well. Many married couples, for example, hit points in their relationships where they realize that things have changed and that they
need to renew their commitment to each other. College students, too,
will inevitably hit that point in their education when they ask, "Is this
right for me? Am I up to this?" Many people raise similar questions in
their jobs. It can be useful under these kinds of circumstances to pray
specifically about this life stage so that we can come to greater clarity
about how to amend our way of living while remaining in our studies,
jobs, or marriages. Many of the hints above apply to this kind of decision. The key theme is to see your decision in "the big picture," meaning as one choice in the midst of a whole life. If the decision is to be a
good one, it must reflect the larger ideal of seeking God in all things
and arranging one's life according to God's will.

Meditating on the Two Powers

In his final address to the Israelites before his death, Moses charged
his people to follow the Lord all of their days:

> *If you obey the commandments of the LORD your God which I com-
> mand you this day, by loving the LORD your God, by walking in his
> ways, and by keeping his commandments and his statutes and his
> ordinances, then you shall live and multiply, and the LORD your
> God will bless you in the land which you are entering to take posses-
> sion of it. But if your heart turns away, and you will not hear, but*

*are drawn away to worship other gods and serve them, I declare to
you this day, that you shall perish; you shall not live long in the land
which you are going over the Jordan to enter and possess. I call
heaven and earth to witness against you this day, that I have set
before you life and death, blessing and curse; therefore choose life,
that you and your descendants may live, loving the* LORD *your God,
obeying his voice, and cleaving to him; for that means life to you
and length of days, that you may dwell in the land which the* LORD
*swore to your fathers, to Abraham, to Isaac, and to Jacob, to give
them. (Dt 30:16–20)*

Moses had led his people for forty years in the desert and knew the
temptations that they faced to abandon God when things were difficult. He had seen their tendency toward idolatry, as in the story when
they constructed and worshiped a golden calf while Moses was on
Mount Sinai. So Moses wanted to leave them with a clear understanding that God alone was the source of their well-being and that any
short-term solution to their problems that did not come from God
was to be avoided.

In our age, we face the same temptations that the Israelites faced in
the desert. We, too, face periods in our lives, both as individuals and
as a society, when our suffering leads us to decisions that are not for
our ultimate well-being. Moses' words are relevant to us, too: we face
a decision between life and death, between blessing and curse. To
choose life may indeed mean choosing the chance for more suffering,
but in the end, it means choosing goodness.

In considering our life decisions, the most poignant conflict we must
confront is between our desire for material prosperity and our desire for
eternal well-being. This is ultimately a conflict of power: do we choose
to give power over to God, meaning we do not have full control of our
life decisions, or do we choose to keep power for ourselves by seeking all
the financial means to control our choices? Jesus said:

*No one can serve two masters; for a slave will either hate the one
and love the other, or be devoted to the one and despise the other.
You cannot serve God and wealth. (Mt 6:24 NRSV)*

Later Jesus said:

> *Consider the lilies of the field, how they grow; they neither toil nor spin; yet I tell you, even Solomon in all his glory was not arrayed like one of these. But if God so clothes the grass of the field, which today is alive and tomorrow is thrown into the oven, will he not much more clothe you, O men of little faith? Therefore do not be anxious, saying, "What shall we eat?" or "What shall we drink?" or "What shall we wear?" For the Gentiles seek all these things; and your heavenly Father knows that you need them all. But seek first his kingdom and his righteousness, and all these things shall be yours as well. Therefore do not be anxious about tomorrow, for tomorrow will be anxious for itself. Let the day's own trouble be sufficient for the day. (Mt 6:28–34)*

It is possible to read Jesus' words in an extreme sense, by rejecting money altogether, like St. Francis of Assisi did after his conversion. Ignatius, too, took a radical view of poverty, following the counsel of Jesus that whoever wants to be perfect should sell everything, give the money to the poor, and follow him. It is illustrative, though, that later in his life, Ignatius spent a good deal of energy deliberating on the place of poverty in the Christian life. He was concerned with the growth of his order and had to determine whether they might more fully live the Gospel by having money or rejecting it altogether. Ignatius's reflections on poverty give us insight into how his order sought to resolve this conflict:

The Advantages of Having a Fixed Income
- It seems that the Society, by having a fixed income, would maintain itself better.
- Having a fixed income, the members would not be annoying or dissatisfying to others by having to beg, especially since those begging would be priests.

- Having a fixed income, they will not experience so many anxieties about begging.
- They will be able to devote themselves better to their duties and prayers.

The Disadvantages of Having a Fixed Income
- The Society receives greater spiritual strength and greater devotion by resembling and contemplating Jesus, our Creator and Lord, so poor and in so many adversities.
- Not to desire any assured income better puts to shame all worldly greed.
- It seems that we are united to the church with greater affection, by being uniform in not having anything ourselves while we are contemplating Christ poor in the sacrament of the Eucharist.
- This helps more to humble us and unite us with the One who humbled himself the most, beyond all others.[1]

In these deliberations, Ignatius shows us how he and his brothers sought to choose between two conflicting visions of power, to choose what was the more authentic response to the will of God. What is important in these deliberations is that Ignatius sought to know which decision would give greater glory to God. Notice that there are strong arguments on both sides; by framing the decision in this way, one could argue convincingly that either choice could be a way to respond to God. Perhaps the more fundamental choice, between life and death, was earlier: whether or not to even bring this deliberation on money into prayer at all.

The very act of bringing a life decision into prayer is an act of faith, even if the decision is unclear. To seek to respond to God in our life choices is difficult. But even if our decisions are not certain, the very attempt to please God is, as Thomas Merton said, itself pleasing to God. This is the real issue in meditating on the two powers: do we choose to let God guide our decisions, or do we choose to handle them ourselves? Perhaps the imagery of a cosmic battle between God and the devil can be described as the choice that human beings make to let God be their guide or to ignore God.

In the popular imagination, there is a belief that when we are faced with tough decisions, we have an angel on one shoulder telling us one thing and a little demon on the other shoulder telling us something different. On a larger scale, many conceive of world history in a similar fashion: the powers of good on one side and the powers of evil on the other. The battleground is humanity itself. There are secret agents on both sides, using their tricks to sway people one way or the other, toward God or toward the devil. These are strong images, which Ignatius himself used to get people to confront their fundamental orientation in life, as did Moses centuries earlier. For us today, there is a similar decision. Whom do we decide to let have power over our life decisions? Do we choose to let God be God, or do we seek to make God into something limited, impotent, and tame? For if God is truly God, then no life decision we make (no decision of any sort, for that matter) is outside God's ability to help us.

Meditating on the Three Types of Persons

There are three ways people can respond to the meditation on power. Imagine three people, each of whom has been given several million dollars. Imagine further that each of these people is basically good—none seeks to do immoral things with the money.

The first person—the postponer—likes the idea of doing God's will but believes that when the time is right, God will show her what to do. She's young and rich, and there is so much life to experience! She rationalizes that God would surely want her to enjoy life—didn't God create life for us to enjoy it? She takes trips, she makes friends, she stays healthy and fit. She invests the money so that it won't be spent in a short time. For her, God is the one to thank for all the good things in life. The thought of giving away all the money because it distracts her from really knowing God is the furthest thing from her mind. As a churchgoer, she knows the biblical accounts of how wealth and God don't mix. She knows "it is easier for a camel to go through the eye of a needle than for a rich man to enter the kingdom of God" (Mt 19:24), but she's also smart and knows that biblical critics have explained that this hyperbole was simply a description of a gate in Jerusalem and that no one should take it too literally. She believes that God must want her to have the money. For her, God's power is very limited—she won't allow God to suggest that there are places to give away her money that would bring others greater joy and lead her into even greater happiness at serving others.

The second person—the compromiser—wants to do the will of God but is so attached to the idea of having money that he simply is not willing to give it up. Over the course of his life, he wrestles with how to serve God, as long as it involves having money. He gives a good deal to charity; he tries to invest in ways that are just, avoiding stock in companies that employ slave-wage labor overseas, or market tobacco to children, or use pornography in their advertising. In short, he does a great deal of good, but he also draws pleasure from being rich and having the kind of power that comes with it. For this person, God's power is limited because he will let God direct only those choices that come with keeping the money.

The third person—the listener—doesn't care if God wants her to keep the money or give it away: she is the perfect example of openness. She just wants to do what God wants. She looks for ways to use the money to relieve the suffering around her. She brings this intention into prayer every day and begins to discern ways that she can continue to help people in various ways. For her, God's power is obvious and constant: through listening to her conscience, she sees many ways to change the world around her.

Now consider the following parable:

[Of the reign of God, Jesus said,] "It will be as when a man going on a journey called his servants and entrusted to them his property; to one he gave five talents, to another two, to another one, to each according to his ability. Then he went away. He who had received the five talents went at once and traded with them; and he made

*five talents more. So also, he who had the two talents made two tal-
ents more. But he who had received the one talent went and dug in
the ground and hid his master's money. Now after a long time the
master of those servants came and settled accounts with them. And
he who had received the five talents came forward, bringing five
talents more, saying, 'Master, you delivered to me five talents; here I
have made five talents more.' His master said to him, 'Well done,
good and faithful servant; you have been faithful over a little, I will
set you over much; enter into the joy of your master.' And he also
who had the two talents came forward, saying, 'Master, you delivered to me two talents; here I have made two talents more.' His
master said to him, 'Well done, good and faithful servant; you have
been faithful over a little, I will set you over much; enter into the
joy of your master.' He also who had received the one talent came
forward, saying, 'Master, I knew you to be a hard man, reaping
where you did not sow, and gathering where you did not winnow;
so I was afraid, and I went and hid your talent in the ground. Here
you have what is yours.' But his master answered him, 'You wicked
and slothful servant! You knew that I reap where I have not sowed,
and gather where I have not winnowed? Then you ought to have
invested my money with the bankers, and at my coming I should
have received what was my own with interest. So take the talent
from him, and give it to him who has the ten talents. For to every
one who has will more be given, and he will have abundance; but
from him who has not, even what he has will be taken away. And
cast the worthless servant into the outer darkness; there men will
weep and gnash their teeth.'" (Mt 25:14–30)*

To the extent that we have invested our power in life in doing God's
will, we are like the first servant, bringing great returns on the
Master's investment. If we keep God's gifts to ourselves, though, we
are worthless. Let us think of money, then, as a potential good; the
extent to which we use our money to create goodness around us is our
investment in our ultimate well-being.

Meditating on the Three Ways of Being Humble

Humility is the gift of readiness to hand over power to God. It is a difficult virtue to practice, especially in a society that extols the rugged individual. But it is necessary if we are to allow God's power to manifest itself in our lives.

Consider three ways of being humble, of allowing God to have power over our lives. The first is the most basic: it involves choosing always to obey God's will, even if it means giving up the power to rule the world. I would not choose to cut off my relationship with God for anything.

The second is more perfect. I choose to obey God always, and moreover, I am indifferent to the ways that God is calling me to live. I don't care about being rich or poor, healthy or sick, popular or obscure. I just want to do whatever God asks me to do, whenever. I would never even consider the slightest action that might harm my relationship with God.

The third way is a radical call to humility, seldom practiced. It involves both the first and second ways of being humble and then more. It involves wanting to imitate Christ and thus deliberately choosing poverty and humiliation out of love for God, to avoid any hint of pride that might distract me.

It is important to recognize that this third way of being humble is not common because it seems counterintuitive, especially in our culture of inflated (and often misguided) self-love. I am struck by it, even as I recognize that it is not something I am able to choose for my own life. Juliana of Norwich, a fourteenth-century mystic, is an example of this approach to humility. She asked God for suffering, even a deathly illness, so that she might more fully be united to Christ. When I read her book *Showings,* I am moved by her complete devotion; there is clearly no other motivating force in her life other than the love of God.

We need to be challenged by this kind of devotion, which is why the meditation on the third type of humility is valuable. We must confront why we need money and health and a certain amount of power, so that we can see these things as means to the end of God's will rather than as ends in themselves. As a husband and father, I know that my responsibilities to my family entail the need for a certain amount of money, health, and power, and I see them as means of responding to God—they are part of God's call to the vocation of married life. But I always face the tension of discerning *how* much power, *how* much money we need, and confronting the third way of being humble reminds me that these things are still only means to a greater end.

We make choices throughout our lives that make us confront the divisions within ourselves. Needing money for very legitimate life purposes always means that we will experience tension, for it is always possible to want more money than we actually need. Do we choose to take a vacation or to help the starving poor in Sudan? Do we choose to buy new clothes or donate to the Red Cross? Do we buy a great cappuccino or give our spare change to a homeless person? The point is that money and power always face us with conflicts. There are two extremes: the first is to avoid them altogether by taking a radical approach to humility and never enjoying money or power. The second is to ignore the conflict and simply enjoy money and power all the time, like the first type of person, the postponer. Most of us are caught in the middle—we experience the tension. But experiencing this tension, wrestling with it constantly, is attending to God's will. The tension itself is good; it is a sign that we care about what God is calling us to do.

THE VOCATION OF CHRIST

For Christians, the model of obedience to the will of God is Jesus the Christ. In discerning the way God calls us to live, we can learn by meditating on the stories of Jesus' life. In this section of the second workout, the objective is to pay attention to the way Jesus made choices that glorified God, in order that we may apply these observations to our own lives. As earlier, put yourself in these stories, and use your imagination. Pay attention to what your own reactions to the characters in the stories tell you about yourself, about Jesus, and about God. It is best to do only one meditation per day, perhaps more than once.

Baptism

Then Jesus appeared: he came from Galilee to the Jordan to be baptized by John. John tried to dissuade him, with the words, "It is I who need baptism from you, and yet you come to me!" But Jesus replied, "Leave it like this for the time being; it is fitting that we should, in this way, do all that uprightness demands." Then John gave in to him.

And when Jesus had been baptized he at once came up from the water, and suddenly the heavens opened and he saw the Spirit of God descending like a dove and coming down on him. And suddenly there was a voice from heaven, "This is my Son, the Beloved; my favor rests on him." (Mt 3:13–17 NJB)

Picture the scene: first as an onlooker, then as John the Baptist, then as Jesus. Pay attention to what strikes you as the scene unfolds. Consider why Jesus answered John the way that he did. What does this tell you about Jesus? What does this mean for the way that Jesus viewed his own vocation?

Temptation in the Desert

And Jesus, full of the Holy Spirit, returned from the Jordan, and was led by the Spirit for forty days in the wilderness, tempted by the devil. And he ate nothing in those days; and when they were ended, he was hungry. The devil said to him, "If you are the Son of God, command this stone to become bread." And Jesus answered him, "It is written, 'Man shall not live by bread alone.'" And the devil took him up, and showed him all the kingdoms of the world in a moment of time, and said to him, "To you I will give all this authority and their glory; for it has been delivered to me, and I give it to whom I will. If you, then, will worship me, it shall all be yours." And Jesus answered him, "It is written, 'You shall worship the Lord your God, and him only shall you serve.'" And he took him to Jerusalem, and set him on the

pinnacle of the temple, and said to him, "If you are the Son of God,
throw yourself down from here; for it is written, 'He will give his
angels charge of you, to guard you,' and 'On their hands they will
bear you up, lest you strike your foot against a stone.'" And Jesus
answered him, "It is said, 'You shall not tempt the Lord your God.'"
And when the devil had ended every temptation, he departed from
him until an opportune time. (Lk 4:1–13)

This is a story ripe for the imagination. Notice first that Jesus is led by the Holy Spirit into the wilderness. Why do you think God would lead Jesus there? What is to be found in the wilderness?

Anyone who has gone on an extended camping trip might have an idea. In the wilderness, there is no distraction; there is only very basic living. One must find food in order to survive, and one must use the simple resources available. It is very easy for the mind to wander when it is not distracted by the many noises we experience in daily living: TV, radio, traffic, advertising, work demands, other people, and so on. When all of those distractions are eliminated, we are faced with the most basic existential questions: What am I doing here? Why do I exist at all? It was confrontation with these questions that tempted Jesus. Note that John has already baptized Jesus, and in that scene, we see a man who is already conscious of his being chosen by God for some purpose. In the wilderness, though, he confronts the devil, who tempts him to misuse his chosenness, to use the power for his own purposes rather than for God's.

As you imagine the scene, consider the ways the devil might tempt you. How are you tempted to misuse the power in your life? What, in your experience, distracts you from doing what God wills? In your prayer, ask God to help you see these distractions and to help you answer in ways similar to the ways Jesus did in the story.

Finally, note the last line of this story: "when the devil had ended every temptation, he departed from him until an opportune time." What do you think Luke was trying to tell us with this line? What is "an opportune time" in Jesus' story or in your own story? When might the devil decide it's a good time to show up again?

Call of the Disciples

While the crowd was pressing in on Jesus and listening to the word of God, he was standing by the Lake of Gennesaret. He saw two boats there alongside the lake; the fishermen had disembarked and were washing their nets. Getting into one of the boats, the one belonging to Simon, he asked him to put out a short distance from the shore. Then he sat down and taught the crowds from the boat. After he had finished speaking, he said to Simon, "Put out into deep water and lower your nets for a catch." Simon said in reply, "Master, we have worked hard all night and have caught nothing, but at your command I will lower the nets." When they had done this, they caught a great number of fish and their nets were tearing. They signaled to their partners in the other boat to come to help them. They came and filled both boats so that they were in danger of sinking. When Simon Peter saw this, he fell at the knees of Jesus and said, "Depart from me, Lord, for I am a sinful man." For astonishment at the catch of fish they had made seized him and all those with him, and likewise James and John, the sons of Zebedee, who were partners of Simon. Jesus said to Simon, "Do not be afraid; from now on you will be catching men." When they brought their boats to the shore, they left everything and followed him. (Lk 5:1–11 NAB)

Here we see Jesus as a public figure, one who arouses the curiosity of those who wish to listen to him. After Jesus gets into the boat of Simon (later called Peter), he teaches the crowds. This suggests that there was a fairly large number of people, for it seems that teaching from the boat was the only way to let everyone hear him well. Here Jesus is already a local celebrity.

One of the things I find interesting about this story is that Jesus does not just say thanks to Simon and then return to shore. As a celebrity, he could have ignored Simon; instead, he spends time with him. Put yourself in the place of Simon in this story: What is your reaction as Jesus is teaching and later when Jesus tells you to head back out to sea? Why do you decide to leave everything and follow Jesus? You've got a prosperous business, with your own boat and a couple of people working with you, and many would say you're a fool to give that all up. What do you imagine happens between you and Jesus that enables you to leave everything behind just to be near him? Can you imagine that happening to you in your own life?

The Beatitudes

When he saw the crowds, he went up the mountain, and after he had sat down, his disciples came to him. He began to teach them, saying:

"Blessed are the poor in spirit,
  for theirs is the kingdom of heaven.
Blessed are they who mourn,
  for they will be comforted.
Blessed are the meek,
  for they will inherit the land.
Blessed are they who hunger and thirst for righteousness,
  for they will be satisfied.
Blessed are the merciful,
  for they will be shown mercy.
Blessed are the clean of heart,
  for they will see God.
Blessed are the peacemakers,
  for they will be called children of God.
Blessed are they who are persecuted for the sake of righteousness,
  for theirs is the kingdom of heaven.

Blessed are you when they insult you and persecute you and utter every kind of evil against you [falsely] because of me." (Mt 5:1–11 NAB)

It may be helpful to dwell on these words of Jesus slowly. Pay attention to each of the "blessed's" in turn by dwelling on the phrase and considering what you think it means in your own life. In what way is your own spirit impoverished? For whom or what do you mourn? Consider the paradox of what Jesus is saying in these statements and how they suggest how different are the ways of God from the ways of people. As an example, the last statement seems difficult to reconcile—no one particularly wants to be insulted. But recall the third way of being humble described above: seeking poverty and humiliation in imitation of Christ and thereby learning to depend wholly on the love of God. Such a person is blessed, says Jesus.

Jesus' words here suggest that being blessed is different from

Being happy
Being satisfied
Being free
Being powerful

Notice that we tend to regard these things as generally good and worth seeking. But Jesus tells us that blessedness is closer to "the kingdom of heaven." Recall the first principle and foundation, which reminds us that our common notions of the good life are only means to the greater end of God's will. This is good news! It is so easy to think of ourselves as being worthless when we feel down. But Jesus offers us a different standard: we are not losers if we are poor, or if we have experienced loss, or if we try to avoid misusing our power, or if others think we are pushovers. Instead, Jesus promises, God sees us through the eyes of creative love.

Consider the ways in which you find your own priorities different from those that seem to be extolled in our culture today. As you consider the list of beatitudes, try to see the ways that they do and do not apply to your life. What do your observations tell you about how you respond to God?

On the Sea

On that day, as evening drew on, he said to them, "Let us cross to the other side." Leaving the crowd, they took him with them in the boat just as he was. And other boats were with him. A violent squall came up and waves were breaking over the boat, so that it was already filling up. Jesus was in the stern, asleep on a cushion. They woke him and said to him, "Teacher, do you not care that we are perishing?" He woke up, rebuked the wind, and said to the sea, "Quiet! Be still!" The wind ceased and there was great calm. Then he asked them, "Why are you terrified? Do you not yet have faith?" They were filled with great awe and said to one another, "Who then is this whom even wind and sea obey?" (Mk 4:35–41 NAB)

Here again is a scene for the imagination. Put yourself on the boat and pay attention to your emotional reactions to the storm and Jesus' response to it. What are your feelings toward Jesus before and after the incident?

The storm is a powerful metaphor for our own lives. What events in your experience were like a storm? Have you ever felt anger at God in a way that made you say, like the disciples, "Don't you care that I'm dying here?" Jesus' response to the disciples seems almost flippant or patronizing, like a parent to a child. Why do you think Jesus responded the way he did?

This story helps me to see past experiences a little differently. In the midst of difficult life situations, there are often fear and feelings of hopelessness. I remember when I was fourteen and had several knee injuries that eventually led to surgery. At the time, it felt like a lot to handle. I was scared at the prospect of surgery, worried about my long-term health and ability to do what I loved—playing sports. It was a dark period, and I wondered if I would ever get out of it. As I look back on that experience now, I can identify with that metaphor of a storm—in the midst of the problems, it seemed like my world was crashing down. I can't even say that I felt that moment where God came in and cleared up everything, as the story depicts Jesus doing. But now that the time is long past, I can see that this was a period of spiritual growth, even though I was unaware of it.

As I ponder the story of Jesus calming the storm, what strikes me is his comment after his rebuke to the wind. "Why are you terrified?" he asks the disciples, as if to suggest that their fear was a lack of faith. The storms in our lives are unavoidable; everyone faces them at different times, and so our only freedom is to be found in our response to them. For Jesus, the disciples' fear during the storm showed an immature understanding of God. For us, the despair that creeps in during life troubles may be a similar failure to understand our ultimate well-being and God's care for it during those times. Knowing this doesn't make our suffering any easier, but it does give us a certain freedom to see suffering as a place where God is still present. Perhaps God will calm the storm, perhaps not; but whether the storm rages or calms, God is still present to us and concerned for our ultimate well-being.

The Miracle at Cana

On the third day there was a wedding in Cana in Galilee, and the mother of Jesus was there. Jesus and his disciples were also invited to the wedding. When the wine ran short, the mother of Jesus said to him, "They have no wine." [And] Jesus said to her, "Woman, how does your concern affect me? My hour has not yet come." His mother said to the servers, "Do whatever he tells you." Now there were six stone water jars there for Jewish ceremonial washings, each holding twenty to thirty gallons. Jesus told them, "Fill the jars with water."

*So they filled them to the brim. Then he told them, "Draw some
out now and take it to the headwaiter." So they took it. And when
the headwaiter tasted the water that had become wine, without
knowing where it came from (although the servers who had drawn
the water knew), the headwaiter called the bridegroom and said to
him, "Everyone serves good wine first, and then when people have
drunk freely, an inferior one; but you have kept the good wine until
now." Jesus did this as the beginning of his signs in Cana in Galilee
and so revealed his glory, and his disciples began to believe in him.
(Jn 2:1–11 NAB)*

I have been struck by this Gospel story ever since I first read Fyodor
Dostoevsky's grand novel *The Brothers Karamazov,* in which there is a
key chapter titled "Cana of Galilee." In John's Gospel, this is the first
miracle that Jesus performs, and so it has great symbolic meaning. For
Dostoevsky, and for his main character, Alyosha, this story represents
an important theme in the spiritual life: Jesus' willingness to share in
and continue the joy of the wedding banquet. It is, I think, the best
example of Jesus' participation in everything that it means to be a
human being. One might argue that the miracle is frivolous: Why
doesn't Jesus use this kind of power to change stones into bread so
that more poor people could eat? Why doesn't he change sand into
gold, to contribute to good causes? Why does he make wine, which
the wedding guests have already been drinking for some time, especially since this probably means they will get drunk?

In Dostoevsky's book, Alyosha is a novice monk who finds himself
imaginatively meditating on the story of Cana: "Ah, that miracle! Ah,
that sweet miracle! It was not men's grief, but their joy Christ visited,
He worked His first miracle to help men's gladness. . . . 'He who loves
men loves their gladness, too.'"[2] Those whose image of God is of a
distant, disinterested being who is not involved in the intimate lives of
people will find this idea different. As you imagine the scene, try to
apply all your senses. Remember that this is likely a group of poor
people having a modest celebration of man and woman beginning
their life together. Picture Jesus, a bit immature still but prodded by

his mom to pitch in. Imagine the temerity of Mary, who probably has an idea of what needs to happen and isn't afraid to let her son know about it! Imagine the parents of the bride, probably embarrassed and humbled by the lack of money to provide enough wine for the guests. Pay attention to the more obnoxious guests, who are already making snide comments about the party running out of wine. Then imagine how the scene changes and how all these characters change. Pay attention to Jesus, who has just done something to keep the party going for hours longer. What is he doing? Why is he doing it?

The Raising of Lazarus

[Jesus said,] "Our friend Lazarus is asleep, but I am going to awaken him." So the disciples said to him, "Master, if he is asleep, he will be saved." But Jesus was talking about his death, while they thought that he meant ordinary sleep. So then Jesus said to them clearly, "Lazarus has died. And I am glad for you that I was not there, that you may believe. Let us go to him." . . .

When Martha heard that Jesus was coming, she went to meet him; but Mary sat at home. Martha said to Jesus, "Lord, if you had been here, my brother would not have died. [But] even now I know that whatever you ask of God, God will give you." Jesus said to her, "Your brother will rise." Martha said to him, "I know he will rise, in the resurrection on the last day." Jesus told her, "I am the resurrection and the life; whoever believes in me, even if he dies, will live, and everyone who lives and believes in me will never die. Do you believe this?" She said to him, "Yes, Lord. I have come to believe that you are the Messiah, the Son of God, the one who is coming into the world."

When she had said this, she went and called her sister Mary secretly, saying, "The teacher is here and is asking for you." . . . When Mary came to where Jesus was and saw him, she fell at his feet and said to him, "Lord, if you had been here, my brother would not have died." When Jesus saw her weeping and the Jews who had come with her weeping, he became perturbed and deeply

troubled, and said, "Where have you laid him?" They said to him,
"Sir, come and see." And Jesus wept. . . .

So Jesus, perturbed again, came to the tomb. It was a cave, and a
stone lay across it. Jesus said, "Take away the stone." Martha, the
dead man's sister, said to him, "Lord, by now there will be a stench;
he has been dead for four days." Jesus said to her, "Did I not tell you
that if you believe you will see the glory of God?" So they took away
the stone. And Jesus raised his eyes and said, "Father, I thank you
for hearing me. I know that you always hear me; but because of the
crowd here I have said this, that they may believe that you sent me."
And when he had said this, he cried out in a loud voice, "Lazarus,
come out!" The dead man came out, tied hand and foot with burial
bands, and his face was wrapped in a cloth. So Jesus said to them,
"Untie him and let him go." (Jn 11:11–44 NAB)

The raising of Lazarus happens not long before Jesus himself is
arrested and sentenced to death. It is a paradox, then, that Jesus shows
his power over death and then refuses to use it for himself. What is he
trying to do, then, by performing this miracle? For if death is something so evil, why did he not choose to stay alive himself? Or why did
he not raise others from the dead? On the other hand, why did he
raise Lazarus from the dead when he knew that Lazarus would have to
die again someday?

It is very telling that Jesus himself is moved to tears at his friend's
death and at the grief of Lazarus's sisters. This is no act; Jesus is not
just moving from place to place performing miracles while remaining
aloof from the rest of humanity. Jesus is a man who cries with his
friends when they lose someone dear to them, even as he knows that
God is going to use the event as a sign. By this point, he has complete
trust in the Father and knows how much the Father loves his people
tenderly: "What father among you, if his son asks for a fish, will
instead of a fish give him a serpent; or if he asks for an egg, will give
him a scorpion? If you then, who are evil, know how to give good
gifts to your children, how much more will the heavenly Father give
the Holy Spirit to those who ask him!" (Lk 11:11–13). As in the story
of Cana, Jesus knows how much God seeks to comfort people and to

give them hope, even to the point of giving them more than they need. God is a prodigal Father, the Good Shepherd who gives his life for his sheep, the Holy Spirit sent to comfort us in our trials. Jesus has internalized this understanding and knows that raising Lazarus will be a sign for people to believe in God.

Lazarus will die again, and Jesus himself will die soon. With this act, Jesus manifests a truth deeper than even our fear of death: our hopefulness that death does not mean annihilation. Lazarus has died, and Lazarus has returned. Can death mean annihilation if one can come back from death? We think of death as a one-way door; Jesus shows us that it is actually a two-way door. Perhaps no one comes back because what is on the other side is so intensely joyful that there is no need to return.

I wish we could speak to Lazarus to learn what he experienced. I wish that John, the writer of the story, gave us some details about what happened to Lazarus after the story. I want to know whether Lazarus felt like he had awakened, as if from a long sleep, or whether he remembered anything from the four days he was dead. How did it change him? Did he see or speak to anyone? Did he see God, or a light?

There are no details. What we see in John's story is Jesus raising Lazarus, then the Sanhedrin plotting to kill Jesus, and the story moves on from there. What is John hinting at? Perhaps that when it comes to considering our salvation, death is simply not of great consequence. It is indeed something we must all face, and for that, Jesus expresses his sympathy, his suffering with us. It is something that qualifies our existence as we know it; it gives us a timeline, a finitude, a limit to how we can live with our choices and relationships. But what is more important is that Jesus, because of his oneness with the Father, has power over death and thus renders it impotent. I am mindful of the words of the seventeenth-century poet John Donne:

Death, be not proud, though some have called thee
Mighty and dreadful, for thou art not so;
For those whom thou think'st thou dost overthrow,
Die not, poor Death, nor yet canst thou kill me.[3]

Jesus raises Lazarus to show the insignificance of death, then chooses to go to his own death, to show the need for it.

Palm Sunday

When they drew near to Jerusalem, to Bethphage and Bethany at the Mount of Olives, he sent two of his disciples and said to them, "Go into the village opposite you, and immediately on entering it, you will find a colt tethered on which no one has ever sat. Untie it and bring it here. If anyone should say to you, 'Why are you doing this?' reply, 'The Master has need of it and will send it back here at once.'" So they went off and found a colt tethered at a gate outside on the street, and they untied it. Some of the bystanders said to them, "What are you doing, untying the colt?" They answered them just as Jesus had told them to, and they permitted them to do it. So they brought the colt to Jesus and put their cloaks over it. And he sat on it. Many people spread their cloaks on the road, and others spread leafy branches that they had cut from the fields. Those preceding him as well as those following kept crying out:

"Hosanna!
   Blessed is he who comes in the name of the Lord!
   Blessed is the kingdom of our father David that is to come!
Hosanna in the highest!"

He entered Jerusalem and went into the temple area. He looked around at everything and, since it was already late, went out to Bethany with the Twelve. (Mk 11:1–11 NAB)

Every year, we read this text at the Mass of Palm Sunday, reenacting the story by waving palm fronds. Our liturgical practice is an example of imaginative prayer: we put ourselves into the story each year, to walk with Jesus into Jerusalem toward the cross. Every year, we know the story and its ending, just like Jesus. He is without a doubt fully aware that to enter Jerusalem is to sign his own death warrant, and yet he does it anyway.

The great paradox in this story is that Jesus seems so universally hailed as a great figure, one who "comes in the name of the Lord." Where are all these people when Jesus is on trial? When I hold my palm, I wonder what might have been my response if I were there at Jesus' entry. Would I have believed in him enough to protest his crucifixion? Would I have cared enough to even follow him after that point, or would I have just treated the event as an interesting publicity stunt, then moved on?

I imagine what Jesus must have felt. Entering Jerusalem to such adulation must have felt wonderful! I wonder whether he felt cynical at the whole thing though, having some sense that these people would say nothing when the Sanhedrin came to arrest him. I wonder whether, after the event, he felt alone, discouraged, afraid, or simply numb. How could he face going to the very place where he knew his enemies were after him?

Facing death so squarely meant that Jesus had to have perfect faith in the Father. Jesus could so easily have justified staying away from Jerusalem: there are more people to heal, more people to raise from the dead, more good to do in the world. Surely it was a matter of social justice to stay alive! And yet Jesus goes to Jerusalem. He shows the kind of detachment that many of us can only wonder at: choosing death in response to the will of God, even over choosing to do good in the world by staying alive. It is a paradox. It takes real faith to believe that one's own death is for an ultimate good. Jesus has this faith, and yet we shall see that it does not exempt him from fear, self-doubt, and despair. It is also a paradox that the greatest faith can coexist with these feelings; it is a sign of hope that those of us who feel them may also (perhaps without our knowing it) be truly faithful through them. As we complete this second workout, let us pray that our faith may mirror the faith of Christ so that we can face our own suffering as Christ did.

SUMMARY OF THE SECOND WORKOUT

The second workout is about coming to rely on the example of Jesus Christ as our guide for knowing the will of God in our lives. Because it can be difficult to practice discernment, we need to confront the obstacles we will inevitably face: doubt, distress, laziness, despair, and many others. It is helpful to consider how Jesus himself had to face these obstacles, and so by meditating on Jesus' life, we can begin to understand how he came to do the will of God.

In our own lives, we are faced with many choices. The second workout also helps us to see our choices with greater perspective and to orient our choices around the ways that God calls us to live. By focusing our attention on the ways that God moves in our lives, we can more clearly recognize those choices that serve our ultimate good and avoid the choices that do not. Again, by looking at the ways that Jesus lived, we can gain insight into how he sought to discern his own vocation, to learn how we might similarly discern ours. Walking with Jesus, we confront the sometimes confusing ways that God works; and ultimately, we walk with him to the place where our faith is tested, in confronting death itself. This will be our challenge in the third workout.

EXERCISES IN THE SECOND WORKOUT

There are three stages to the workout. Again, use the seven practices: gaining interior peace; practicing the presence of God; making a preparatory prayer; using your imagination; making your requests known; engaging in a closing conversation with God; and repeating what works for you.

Stage One

The first stage comprises a series of meditations on Jesus' early life. Use only one on a given day, and if one bears fruit, then repeat it.

1. The creation story (Gn 1:1–4)
2. The relationship of the Father and the Son (Jn 1:1–5)
3. The Annunciation (Lk 1:26–31)
4. The birth of Jesus (Lk 2:4–7)
5. The presentation in the temple (Lk 2:22–32)
6. The flight into Egypt (Mt 2:13–14)
7. Finding Jesus in the temple (Lk 2:41–49)

Stage Two

The second stage is a focus on your own discernment process, either about a major life decision coming up or about improving on the life you have already chosen. There are several elements to this part of the workout:

1. Prayer for God's Guidance

Pray for God's guidance about the decision and for knowledge about the way that God is calling you to live your life. Pay attention to your likes, your talents, your hopes, and what you are good at, and ask God how to use these for God's greater glory.

2. Meditation on the Two Powers

Meditate on the two powers: between life and death, between the will of God and the limited ways of the world. Consider the following:

Choosing life by choosing to obey God (Dt 30:16–20)
Serving God or money (Mt 6:24)
Being like the flowers and putting worry aside (Mt 6:28–34)

3. Meditation on the Three Types of Persons

Meditate on the three types of persons: the postponer, the compromiser, and the listener. Pray that God might give you the gift of the

Holy Spirit, in order that you might more fully listen to and do the will of God in your life. Pray for wisdom to know God's will, courage to do God's will, and hope to love God's will. Consider the parable of the talents (Mt 25:14–30).

4. Meditation on the Three Ways of Being Humble

Meditate on the three ways of being humble: obeying God and choosing not to commit a serious sin; obeying God and choosing not to commit any kind of sin; obeying God by seeking suffering. Pray that God might reveal to you the ways to use your power.

Stage Three

The third stage is a series of meditations on the vocation of Christ so that we might more fully understand what perfect obedience to the will of God is like. As you do these meditations, use them to illuminate the choice or choices that you seek to discern in your own life.

1. Baptism (Mt 3:13–17)
2. Temptation in the desert (Lk 4:1–13)
3. Call of the disciples (Lk 5:1–11)
4. The Beatitudes (Mt 5:3–12)
5. On the sea (Mk 4:35–41)
6. The miracle at Cana (Jn 2:1–11)
7. The raising of Lazarus (Jn 11:20–44)
8. Palm Sunday (Mk 11:1–11)

7

third workout:
walking with Christ

AS I WRITE THESE WORDS I AM MINDFUL OF MY EXPERIENCE OF HOLY
Week, which just concluded a few days ago. I have consistently found
that the way Christians observe this week is a good example of imaginative liturgical prayer: we suspend our experience about the everyday
world and imagine ourselves walking with Christ into Jerusalem,
through the Last Supper, into the Garden of Gethsemane, and toward
death. Many hold the Triduum, the three days before the celebration
of Easter, as the most solemn part of the year, for in these days, we
imagine ourselves participating in the very death of Christ.

The observance of Holy Week parallels what Ignatius directs in the third workout. By contemplating the passion and death of Jesus, we come to a fuller appreciation of what this fundamental mystery means for our own lives. Moreover, we imaginatively respond to Christ's invitation to be with him, as spoken in Gethsemane: "Stay here, and keep watch with me." Having examined our own lives in the first workout and having meditated on the life of Christ as our model in the second workout, now we are ready to enter into Christ's suffering as a friend, bearing his burdens as our own. As with the first and second workouts, read through the chapter, then pray using the texts listed at the end of the chapter. You can use the meditations on the texts that I offer in the chapter or simply use the same practice you have developed in the first two workouts on your own.

The third workout challenges us to use what we gained from the meditation on the two powers in the second workout. Choosing to follow Christ means choosing to share in Christ's suffering, in the hope that we too might share in Christ's resurrection (see Rom 6:5; Phil 3:10–11). This choice mirrors the kind of situation anyone faces in a friendship: to truly love another means taking part in the other's suffering.

There is an existential paradox at the heart of the third workout, then. It is inscribed into the human condition: the fundamental choice either to love or not to love. Even the most basic act of love means reaching out to the other and, in so doing, sacrificing something of oneself, however small. Love, then, means sacrifice; it is a kind of death of self. The paradox is that this is what gives us life, for no one can live exempt from all love. We must love in order to live, and we must die in order to love. The one who loves emerges as a changed person. John Henry Newman put it best: to live is to change, and to live long is to have changed often.

Entering into the third workout readies us for death, in the sense that we will be challenged to embrace Jesus so profoundly as to be ready to serve him even to the point of death. "No one has greater love than this, to lay down one's life for one's friends," he said (Jn 15:13 NAB). In seeking God's will as perfectly as Jesus did, we face the same paradox: we will face death, but in the hope of greater life. Our ultimate well-being can emerge only if we put to death our limited perceptions of what happiness is. Put aside your expectations, one writer put it, and let us change the world.

Confronting the paradox of death and life, though, we face the fear of annihilation. Fear of death, on either the metaphorical or literal level, is natural, it seems. So much of our youth is spent trying to construct our identities, and so the prospect of dying to self seems wrong. Often this tension arises in our relationships: the beloved calls us into a new way of living, and many justify their unwillingness to cooperate by the appeal "That's just not the kind of person I am." It can be hard to overcome this fear. I remember many times when I have been challenged in this way, and what strikes me is how difficult it can be to discern healthy change in one's own life. We do need to die to self, but we don't want to be crushed.

The film *Remember the Titans* is based on the true story of a football team that had to overcome racism to achieve their goal of a championship. It is a moving story of the paradox of death and life on the metaphorical level: these high school–age boys had to overcome their fear and dislike of the others in order to develop trust and camaraderie. They had to put to death the opinions that had been inculcated in them since childhood: namely, that the blacks (or whites) were no good. By the end of the film, it is clear that the players emerged as changed people.

A film that is similar, in that it describes a person's metaphorical death of self, is *Schindler's List*. In this film, also based on a true story, Oskar Schindler is a German businessman during World War II who typifies the person who embraces the first power described in the second workout: he loves money and sees it as the means to his happiness. Over time, he comes to know the humanity of the Jews who worked in his factory, to the extent that he makes a courageous decision to save them from the Nazis. Suffice it to say that the Schindler of the end of the film is a very different person from the Schindler of the beginning: he has undergone a conversion, a death of self, and emerges as a man of great courage and passion.

The difficulty for us today is that courage and passion come at a price. The example of Jesus reminds us that this price is small compared to the end result: God's love. Having walked with our companion, Jesus, through the second workout, let us continue to walk with him through the third. We know, as he did, that there is one end in sight: death. But in our doubt, sorrow, and even despair, let us remind each other of our hope in the Resurrection.

PREPARING FOR THE THIRD WORKOUT

When I lived in Oxford, I spent many days just wandering around the medieval buildings, imagining myself living centuries ago. I was struck by the architecture of the Gothic structures and found it easy to picture groups of monks wandering in and out of the chapels, going about their studies. On many occasions, I sought out performances and liturgical services that involved ancient music, and as I listened, I would let my imagination roam freely about the thirteenth century. To complete the picture, I often attended the Latin Masses that were held at St. Aloysius Church. Just being there seemed to close the distance of time between then and now. I imagined what life as a monk must have been like: prayer and work, all for the love of God.

When Lent came, I was ready to immerse myself in the flow of the season. In Oxford there are so many places with religious symbolism, and so it was very easy to constantly remind myself. I felt myself an actor in an ancient drama: practicing the same rigors as had so many before me, in this place, during this liturgical time. In short, I felt part of something much greater than me, and so I brought to that season a willingness to give every effort to do it right. I was diligent in prayer; I was moved by the constant participation in the sacred liturgy; I was mindful of seeking God in everything; I was careful in my fasting. When the Triduum (Holy Thursday, Good Friday, and Holy Saturday) began, I entered it with an uncommon solemnity: I lived those three days with Jesus in such a way as to bring that time alive to me as never before. When Easter finally arrived, I was genuinely exultant: the freedom of singing alleluia felt like the emergence of springtime after a harsh winter. Even today, many years later, I appreciate the memory of that season.

The third workout is an investment: what we put into our preparation for these meditations will yield great fruit. My Oxford experience taught me about investing in prayer time, even though now I realize that some of it was self-centered. Dramatizing my prayer life helped me to treat it seriously and to see it as something grounded in more than my own whim. Where it became a bit self-centered was in my treating it as a kind of "peak experience," a kind of high, like one gets from traveling or doing exciting things. The third workout is meant to be taken seriously, and it may be helpful to treat it with some drama. But it is not (nor is spirituality in general) an "experience" in the sense of something designed to give us a thrill. It is about seeking the grace to love Christ to the end—his suffering and death—so that we might share in the hope of Christ's resurrection.

About a decade after Oxford, I spent a short but poignant time on retreat at a Trappist monastery. There, too, I chose to immerse myself in the movement of the liturgical season—in this case, by participating in the monastic Liturgy of the Hours, which involves praying the psalms and other texts seven times over a twenty-four-hour period. I recall the prayer in the middle of the night being the most powerful. I set the alarm for 1:45 A.M., awoke, and walked about half a mile to the chapel. There was very little light or sound; the monastery is in the middle of nowhere. I had to bring a flashlight just to walk the path, alone and in silence, and as I did this, I recalled the words of the psalmist: "Your word is a lamp for my feet, / a light for my path" (Ps 119:105 NAB). Praying the psalms was delicious; it was the one break from the complete silence I held during the rest of my time there. In silence, I was able to more clearly listen to God. In praying the psalms, I was able to more clearly articulate my own hunger for God.

I mention all this to underscore that some simple resolutions can help us in our prayer of the third week. What I have gained from my experiences in Oxford and at the monastery is the belief that bringing our whole selves into prayer is of great value. This is not as easy as it sounds. Many people pray only with their heads, or their lips, or their emotions, or their actions. And while all of these are good in themselves, what is best is to let our heads, lips, emotions, actions, and indeed our very hearts, manifest a sincere devotion to prayer all together. When I was younger, dramatizing my prayer helped me to do this. More recently, I find that occasionally I need to completely withdraw from the rest of my life in order to do this. Most people, of course, do not have the time (or inclination) to completely withdraw, and so it is important to learn other ways. Notice that Lent is itself a time when the church as a whole makes a commitment of this sort. Lent is set aside so that all Christians can enter into special preparations for those mysteries at the heart of Christian spirituality. If you are able, use this time to do the third workout. If not, think of other ways you can bring prayer into different facets of your daily routine. Do volunteer work; make an extra effort to reach out to your loved ones; skip a meal and use the money to help a homeless person; read mystical poetry (St. John of the Cross, Gerard Manley Hopkins, John Donne, and George Herbert are a few of my favorites); paint or write about a religious theme; counsel a child; visit your elderly relatives or neighbors. Whatever you do, use it to focus on the theme of dying to self.

The third workout is, by contemporary standards, the most dark. It is not fun to meditate on suffering and death, particularly in a culture such as ours, which has almost completely lost its ability to confront death. I am struck by the practice of the monks of centuries past who would sleep in their coffins every night as a reminder of their ultimate end: "You are dust, and to dust you shall return." Earlier cultures were much more cognizant of death because it was a reality that they regularly confronted before the discoveries of modern hygiene and medicine. It conditioned every part of their lives. In some places, children were not named until they reached a certain age because so many children died young. Mothers often died in childbirth. Men often died before what we would today call middle age. Plagues swept through cities and nations, taking massive numbers of the population. Death was seen as a constant, though unwelcome, reality.

Today, by contrast, we treat death as the ultimate enemy. In every hospital, professionals will talk about how to "beat this," whether it be cancer, heart disease, or the effects of a serious accident. Death must be overcome, as though it were some creeping villain trying to steal us away from where we ought to be.

The by-product of this otherwise understandable attitude is that we often defer confronting the very reality of our own death. Medicine is wonderful, but ultimately it cannot save us from death. Confronting this reality need not be macabre or gothic; it is as normal and obvious as confronting the sunrise. "I am going to die." Is this hard to say? Is this hard to think about? Perhaps more poignantly, we must ask, "Why does God want me to die?" Death is written into the contract for being human, and so we are foolish if we ignore that clause altogether.

Walking with Jesus to his death teaches us a great deal. It is clear from the Gospels that Jesus knows he is going to die, even before the immediate events leading up to his death take place. Yet we see a man firm in his resolve that he need not avoid death. Instead of running away, he actually returns to Jerusalem, as we saw at the end of the second workout—and he does it in a way to attract attention. Yet even in his resolve to face his own death, he is not exempt from emotion. He is terrified; he despairs; he loses hope; he feels alienated from his friends; he feels God has abandoned him. In all this, though, he never loses faith. What this means is that one can be faithful even in the midst of terror, despair, hopelessness, alienation, and feelings of abandonment. What this also means is that death need not crush faith.

Allow yourself to enter into these contemplations with your whole self. If it is possible, maintain an attitude that corresponds to the serious nature of the stories so that you do not have to completely switch emotional gears over the course of the workout. The themes are suffering and death: you are walking with someone you love through this period, so pay attention to the ways your whole self responds to the rest of your world during this time. Remember that the point is not to make ourselves feel bad; instead, it is to express solidarity with Jesus and to ask God for the grace to suffer with him. Read through these meditations, then use the texts listed at the end of the chapter in your prayer.

THE WAY OF THE CROSS

Picture Jesus staying in Bethany, just outside of the city of Jerusalem, when he sends two disciples ahead of him to prepare the Last Supper. He later follows with his other disciples. During this dinner, Jesus washes their feet and offers them bread and wine; these actions he does with great solemnity, and the disciples are perplexed. As we put ourselves in these scenes, let us share in the disciples' feelings: honor to be in the presence of someone we admire; confusion at what these actions mean; fear that Jesus seems to be talking about the end; anguish that so many people misunderstand our Lord and want to kill him.

Consider that Jesus undertakes these actions with so much humility. Here is a man able to cure sickness, heal the blind, raise the dead; he knows the will of God perfectly. Yet he chooses not to exalt himself; he suffers quietly. Imagine that Jesus has chosen to undertake these indignities for you alone; he will go to his death so that your sins might be forgiven. He is God in human flesh; he has the power to avoid this suffering, and yet in solidarity with all of us who suffer, he chooses to let things take their course.

The Foot Washing

Jesus, knowing that the Father had given all things into his hands, and that he had come from God and was going to God, rose from supper, laid aside his garments, and girded himself with a towel. Then he poured water into a basin, and began to wash the disciples' feet, and to wipe them with the towel with which he was girded. He came to Simon Peter; and Peter said to him, "Lord, do you wash my feet?" Jesus answered him, "What I am doing you do not know now, but afterward you will understand." Peter said to him, "You shall never wash my feet." Jesus answered him, "If I do not wash you, you have no part in me." Simon Peter said to him, "Lord, not my feet only but also my hands and my head!" Jesus said to him, "He who has bathed does not need to wash, except for his feet, but he is clean all over; and you are clean, but not every one of you." For he knew who was to betray him; that was why he said, "You are not all clean." When he had washed their feet, and taken his garments, and resumed his place, he said to them, "Do you know what I have done to you? You call me Teacher and Lord; and you are right, for so I am. If I then, your Lord and Teacher, have washed your feet, you also ought to wash one another's feet. For I have given you an example, that you also should do as I have done to you." (Jn 13:3–15)

As you imagine this scene, picture yourself as Peter. What is your response to Jesus when he comes to wash your feet? You have already made a profession of faith in this man: "You are the Messiah of God" (see Lk 9:20). Will you let him wash your feet?

Now picture yourself as Jesus. What do you feel as you enact the scene? How do you respond to the disciples' quizzical looks? Why do you choose to do this?

Ask God to help you understand in your own life Jesus' words: "If I then, your Lord and Teacher, have washed your feet, you also ought to wash one another's feet." What does this mean for you? Whose "feet" are you to wash?

The Last Supper

When it was evening, he sat at table with the twelve disciples; and as they were eating, he said, "Truly, I say to you, one of you will betray me." And they were very sorrowful, and began to say to him one after another, "Is it I, Lord?" He answered, "He who has dipped his hand in the dish with me, will betray me. The Son of man goes as it is written of him, but woe to that man by whom the Son of man is betrayed! It would have been better for that man if he had not been born." Judas, who betrayed him, said, "Is it I, Master?" He said to him, "You have said so." Now as they were eating, Jesus took bread, and blessed, and broke it, and gave it to the

disciples and said, "Take, eat; this is my body." And he took a cup,
and when he had given thanks he gave it to them, saying, "Drink
of it, all of you; for this is my blood of the covenant, which is
poured out for many for the forgiveness of sins. I tell you I shall not
drink again of this fruit of the vine until that day when I drink it
new with you in my Father's kingdom." And when they had sung a
hymn, they went out to the Mount of Olives. (Mt 26:20–30)

For many Christians, the story of the Last Supper is familiar because it is often reenacted. Because of this reason, though, it can be easy to miss what it means. Rituals are good inasmuch as they constantly bring us back into consideration of what the community values; but our tendency can sometimes be to dismiss what we see as repetitious. In imagining the story of the Last Supper, try to approach it as if for the first time. Put yourself in the scene: hear the various conversations of the disciples as Jesus calls their attention. Feel the dismay they feel as Jesus issues a cryptic condemnation. Pay attention to the smell of baked bread, the feel of the hot air in the crowded room, the smell of dust and sweat.

As Jesus turns to Judas, what is your reaction? Are you angry, confused, surprised? Ask yourself why you think Jesus publicly humiliates him as he does. Pay attention to the reactions of the other disciples. Can you imagine what it's like if Jesus is speaking about you?

As you're having dinner with the disciples, what are you talking about? What do you think when Jesus again attracts everyone's attention with the blessing and breaking of bread? Remember that this supper is a celebration of the ancient Passover and that Jesus and his disciples are observing the memory of God's commands to Moses (Ex 24). The Israelites had been told to slaughter a lamb, whose blood would be shed as a holy offering to God. Familiar with this tradition, the apostles are no doubt a little perplexed as to what Jesus means by identifying himself with the bread and wine used in this ritual observance. What is your reaction to Jesus' words "this is my body" and "this is my blood of the covenant"? What are you feeling as you sing a hymn and go to the Mount of Olives?

Gethsemane

Then Jesus came with them to a place called Gethsemane, and he said to his disciples, "Sit here while I go over there and pray." He took along Peter and the two sons of Zebedee, and began to feel sorrow and distress. Then he said to them, "My soul is sorrowful even to death. Remain here and keep watch with me." He advanced a little and fell prostrate in prayer, saying, "My Father, if it is possible, let this cup pass from me; yet, not as I will, but as you will." When he returned to his disciples he found them asleep. He said to Peter, "So you could not keep watch with me for one hour? Watch and pray that you may not undergo the test. The spirit is willing, but the flesh is weak." Withdrawing a second time, he prayed again, "My Father, if it is not possible that this cup pass without my drinking it, your will be done!" Then he returned once more and found them asleep, for they could not keep their eyes open. He left them and withdrew again and prayed a third time, saying the same thing again. Then he returned to his disciples and said to them, "Are you still sleeping and taking your rest? Behold, the hour is at hand when the Son of Man is to be handed over to sinners. Get up, let us go. Look, my betrayer is at hand." (Mt 26:36–46 NAB)

One of my favorite meditative chants is taken from the story of Jesus in Gethsemane: "Stay here and keep watch with me. . . . Watch and pray." The monks of Taizé have set this text to music, repeating Jesus' words over and over again throughout the chant. On different occasions, I have found meditating on this text very moving. We who look back on this story during Holy Week know that it is the preamble to the death of Christ and so convince ourselves that we would stay with him until the end. But the disciples do not have the wisdom of hindsight. They are tired, and perhaps a little selfish, and so let Jesus go off alone while they sleep. His prayer indicates what he is feeling: afraid, yet resolute. His words are a challenge to us today: Can we be with him through his suffering? Are we willing to take on the task of walking with him to the cross? Do we love him enough to not let him be alone through this trial?

The Arrest

While he was still speaking, Judas came, one of the twelve, and with him a great crowd with swords and clubs, from the chief priests and the elders of the people. Now the betrayer had given them a sign, saying, "The one I shall kiss is the man; seize him." And he came up to Jesus at once and said, "Hail, Master!" And he kissed him. Jesus said to him, "Friend, why are you here?" Then they came up and laid hands on Jesus and seized him. And behold, one of those who were with Jesus stretched out his hand and drew his sword, and struck the slave of the high priest, and cut off his ear. Then Jesus said to him, "Put your sword back into its place; for all who take the sword will perish by the sword. Do you think that I cannot appeal to my Father, and he will at once send me more than twelve legions of angels? But how then should the scriptures be fulfilled, that it must be so?" At that hour Jesus said to the crowds, "Have you come out as against a robber, with swords and clubs to capture me? Day after day I sat in the temple teaching, and you did not seize me. But all this has taken place, that the scriptures of the prophets might be fulfilled." Then all the disciples forsook him and fled. (Mt 26:47–56)

The juxtaposition of violence and tenderness in this scene is striking. People with weapons arrest Jesus, the peacemaker, after Judas betrays him with a kiss. A disciple reacts violently, but Jesus heals the slave. What is the slave's reaction? Jesus' words emphasize the paradox: he has power at his disposal but refuses to use it. Why? Why does Jesus not ask the Father to destroy all the sinners, manifest his power and glory, and reward the righteous? His answer is even more mysterious: to fulfill the Scriptures. As a father, I find it hard to imagine letting anyone harm my child without doing something extreme. Where is the Father in this story? Why does he choose to remain absent? At this moment, Jesus is totally alone. The disciples have fled, and he is now in the power of those who wish to see him dead.

Before the Sanhedrin

Then those who had seized Jesus led him to Caiaphas the high priest, where the scribes and the elders had gathered. But Peter followed him at a distance, as far as the courtyard of the high priest, and going inside he sat with the guards to see the end. Now the chief priests and the whole council sought false testimony against Jesus that they might put him to death, but they found none, though many false witnesses came forward. At last two came forward and said, "This fellow said, 'I am able to destroy the temple of God, and to build it in three days.'" And the high priest stood up and said, "Have you no answer to make? What is it that these men testify against you?" But Jesus was silent. And the high priest said to him, "I adjure you by the living God, tell us if you are the Christ, the Son of God." Jesus said to him, "You have said so. But I tell you, hereafter you will see the Son of man seated at the right hand of Power, and coming on the clouds of heaven." Then the high priest tore his robes, and said, "He has uttered blasphemy. Why do we still need witnesses? You have now heard his blasphemy. What is your judgment?" They answered, "He deserves death." Then they spat in his face, and struck him; and some slapped him, saying, "Prophesy to us, you Christ! Who is it that struck you?" (Mt 26:57–68)

The story moves toward its inevitable conclusion: Jesus is going to die. He has done nothing wrong, but those in power see him as a threat. No matter what he says, they are going to see it as evidence of whatever they want to believe. His one oblique comment sends the high priest into a rage and summons the sarcasm of those near him. What can Jesus do or say, now that all around hate him?

I wonder about those unnamed people in the scene. Did they wake up the next day with any recollection of Jesus? Was it just another day at the office? Did they have any personal feeling of Jesus' guilt, or were they just following whatever their leaders told them to believe? As we read this story today, are there similar events of injustice going on under our noses that we are not paying attention to? Is Jesus among us somewhere, suffering unnoticed? We do well to remember what he said to his disciples about the Father, when they protested that they would surely help him if they knew how to do it: "Then they will answer and say, 'Lord, when did we see you hungry or thirsty or a stranger or naked or ill or in prison, and not minister to your needs?' He will answer them, 'Amen, I say to you, what you did not do for one of these least ones, you did not do for me'" (Mt 25:44–45 NAB).

Peter's Denial

Now Peter was sitting outside in the courtyard. And a maid came up to him, and said, "You also were with Jesus the Galilean." But he denied it before them all, saying, "I do not know what you mean." And when he went out to the porch, another maid saw him, and she said to the bystanders, "This man was with Jesus of Nazareth." And again he denied it with an oath, "I do not know the man." After a little while the bystanders came up and said to Peter, "Certainly you are also one of them, for your accent betrays you." Then he began to invoke a curse on himself and to swear, "I do not know the man." And immediately the cock crowed. And Peter remembered the saying of Jesus, "Before the cock crows, you will deny me three times." And he went out and wept bitterly. (Mt 26:69–75)

We would all like to believe that we would not behave in such a cowardly way as Peter. In the end, he wants to save his own skin, rather than admit to following Jesus. This text makes me think of the ways that I can sometimes avoid being labeled "Christian" by hiding what I really believe, going along with the status quo. It is not easy to face ridicule for what one believes.

What is hopeful is that Peter, even in spite of this action, becomes a leader in the early church. God somehow redeems this man; perhaps he can do the same with us. Perhaps even in spite of the times when we have acted the way Peter does, we can witness to our faith in Christ by trying to be more like him. As you pray with this text, ask God to help you see the ways that you manifest your faith and the ways that you hide your faith out of fear.

Before Pontius Pilate

Now Jesus stood before the governor; and the governor asked him, "Are you the King of the Jews?" Jesus said, "You have said so." But when he was accused by the chief priests and elders, he made no answer. Then Pilate said to him, "Do you not hear how many things they testify against you?" But he gave him no answer, not even to a single charge; so that the governor wondered greatly. Now at the feast the governor was accustomed to release for the crowd any one prisoner whom they wanted. And they had then a notorious prisoner, called Barabbas. So when they had gathered, Pilate said to them, "Whom do you want me to release for you, Barabbas or Jesus who is called Christ?" For he knew that it was out of envy that they had delivered him up. Besides, while he was sitting on the judgment seat, his wife sent word to him, "Have nothing to do with that righteous man, for I have suffered much over him today in a dream." Now the chief priests and the elders persuaded the people to ask for Barabbas and destroy Jesus. The governor again said to them, "Which of the two do you want me to release for you?" And they said, "Barabbas." Pilate said to them, "Then what shall I do with Jesus who is called Christ?" They all said, "Let him be crucified." And he said, "Why, what evil has he done?" But they shouted all the more, "Let him be crucified." (Mt 27:11–23)

Matthew's telling of this story is about blame shifting: he wants to show the weakness of the Roman governor and thereby place blame on the crowd, those who are screaming for Jesus' death. Put yourself in the scene. Those who have reenacted the Palm Sunday liturgy, in which the congregation speaks the words of the crowd in this scene, will have some experience doing this. Why do you think the crowd answers so emphatically? It seems that there are times when people are willing to be told what to believe, especially when there is the opportunity to witness some kind of violence. We have a dark side: in German, it is called *Schadenfreude*, literally "injury joy"—that is, the satisfaction of seeing someone else suffer. Perhaps it is because we feel power over the situation, being removed from what the other is going through.

What is your emotional reaction to the words of the crowd? Do you want to react like Peter did and hide? Or do you want to rush to Jesus and tell the crowd they have been duped?

The Crowning with Thorns

Then the soldiers of the governor took Jesus into the praetorium, and they gathered the whole battalion before him. And they stripped him and put a scarlet robe upon him, and plaiting a crown of thorns they put it on his head, and put a reed in his right hand. And kneeling before him they mocked him, saying, "Hail, King of the Jews!" And they spat upon him, and took the reed and struck him on the head. And when they had mocked him, they stripped him of the robe, and put his own clothes on him, and led him away to crucify him. (Mt 27:27–31)

Here again is an example of men who have been told what to believe and act cruelly because of it. We can sometimes rationalize our cruelty by a basic appeal: he or she deserves it. What is unfortunate is that sometimes we aren't even aware of our own cruelty: an offhand remark, a choice that affects people we don't even see, an omission of some responsibility to another. For the soldiers, this was all just good fun—they, too, probably just forgot about it the next day.

But put yourself in Jesus' place. What are your feelings? Are you resigned, resentful, enraged, disconcerted, or simply numb? What do your feelings tell you about Jesus' attitude toward the Father, toward his disciples, toward the soldiers?

The Crucifixion

After they had crucified him, they divided his garments by casting lots; then they sat down and kept watch over him there. And they placed over his head the written charge against him: This is Jesus, the King of the Jews. Two revolutionaries were crucified with him, one on his right and the other on his left. Those passing by reviled him, shaking their heads and saying, "You who would destroy the temple and rebuild it in three days, save yourself, if you are the Son of God, [and] come down from the cross!" Likewise the chief priests with the scribes and elders mocked him and said, "He saved others; he cannot save himself. So he is the king of Israel! Let him come down from the cross now, and we will believe in him. He trusted in God; let him deliver him now if he wants him. For he said, 'I am the Son of God.'" The revolutionaries who were crucified with him also kept abusing him in the same way.

From noon onward, darkness came over the whole land until three in the afternoon. And about three o'clock Jesus cried out in a loud voice, "Eli, Eli, lema sabachthani?" which means, "My God, my God, why have you forsaken me?" (Mt 27:35–46 NAB)

Jesus' words at the end of this text sum up what he is feeling. Matthew chose these words from Psalm 22:2 to describe Jesus' state just before he expires: he has done what the Father asked of him and feels abandoned. Consider how this perfect act of obedience has brought Jesus to a place of utter desolation. Can it be that doing God's will can sometimes leave us feeling hopeless and alone?

Now two others, both criminals, were led away with him to be executed.

When they came to the place called the Skull, they crucified him and the criminals there, one on his right, the other on his left. [Then Jesus said, "Father, forgive them, they know not what they do."] They divided his garments by casting lots. The people stood by and watched; the rulers, meanwhile, sneered at him and said, "He saved others, let him save himself if he is the chosen one, the Messiah of God." Even the soldiers jeered at him. As they approached to offer him wine they called out, "If you are King of the Jews, save yourself." Above him there was an inscription that read, "This is the King of the Jews."

Now one of the criminals hanging there reviled Jesus, saying, "Are you not the Messiah? Save yourself and us." The other, however, rebuking him, said in reply, "Have you no fear of God, for you are subject to the same condemnation? And indeed, we have been condemned justly, for the sentence we received corresponds to our crimes, but this man has done nothing criminal." Then he said, "Jesus, remember me when you come into your kingdom." He replied to him, "Amen, I say to you, today you will be with me in Paradise."

It was now about noon and darkness came over the whole land until three in the afternoon because of an eclipse of the sun. Then the veil of the temple was torn down the middle. Jesus cried out in a loud voice, "Father, into your hands I commend my spirit"; and when he had said this he breathed his last. (Lk 23:32–46 NAB)

Luke's portrayal of the scene is different from Matthew's. For Luke, Jesus seems more convinced of the Father's care through his suffering. He forgives his persecutors and comforts the compassionate criminal by making a promise that he will be with Jesus in heaven. His final breath amounts to a kind of prayer: now that he has completely offered his body to the will of the Father, he offers his spirit as well. In both Greek and Hebrew, the word we translate as "spirit" has the dual meaning of "breath" and referred to what animates the human being. By uttering these words as his breath leaves him, Jesus gives over his very life to the Father, in perfect trust.

This portrait of Jesus gives us a model of trust. It is the image of a dying person who knows that God is there to welcome him; it is hopeful for those (for example) with terminal illness. Matthew's portrait of Jesus is a comfort to those who feel abandoned by God, saying in effect that if God's own Son felt lost, then ordinary Christians need not lose hope when they, too, feel abandoned. As you pray over these different texts, pay attention to which one speaks to your present experience more profoundly.

> *But standing by the cross of Jesus were his mother, and his mother's sister, Mary the wife of Clopas, and Mary Magdalene. When Jesus saw his mother, and the disciple whom he loved standing near, he said to his mother, "Woman, behold, your son!" Then he said to the disciple, "Behold, your mother!" And from that hour the disciple took her to his own home. After this Jesus, knowing that all was now finished, said (to fulfill the scripture), "I thirst." A bowl full of vinegar stood there; so they put a sponge full of the vinegar on hyssop and held it to his mouth. When Jesus had received the vinegar, he said, "It is finished"; and he bowed his head and gave up his spirit. (Jn 19:25–30)*

John's last portrait of Jesus shows an even more dramatized main character. John shows Jesus as one fulfilling his role in perfect obedience to the Father's script. John writes the story to be a kind of bookend: on one side is the story of Cana, when Jesus says, "Woman, how does your concern affect me? My hour has not yet come"; on the other side is this story, in which Jesus says, "Woman, behold, your son!" His hour has indeed come, and he has been preparing for it throughout the ministry that John describes. John's portrait emphasizes a Jesus who enacts the divine drama under the guidance of the Father, and John suggests to his readers that their faithful living is part of that same drama. As you pray with this text, ask God to help you to know your part in this drama.

Mary, His Mother

The figure of Jesus' mother in John's text is especially moving and has captured the imagination of many Christians over the centuries. Here, in the story of Jesus' crucifixion, we see the completion of what the prophet Simeon said when Mary brought Jesus to the temple as an infant: "Behold, this child is set for the fall and rising of many in Israel, and for a sign that is spoken against (and a sword will pierce through your own soul also), that thoughts out of many hearts may be revealed" (Lk 2:34–35). The sacred poem *Stabat Mater*, attributed to the thirteenth-century Franciscan Jacopone da Todi, is about her pain. It is an example of immersing oneself imaginatively into the Gospel story and has been used for centuries as a devotional text:

> *The mother of sorrows stood in tears beside the cross on which her Son was hanging.*
> *Her grieving heart, anguished and lamenting, was pierced by a sword;*
> *How sad and afflicted was that blessed Mother of her only Son,*
> *For she grieved and sorrowed, the pious Mother, as she witnessed the pains of her great Son.*
> *Where is the man who would not weep to see the Mother of Christ in such suffering?*
> *Who would not share her sorrow, seeing the loving Mother grieving with her Son?*
> *For the sins of His people she saw Jesus in torment and subdued with whips.*
> *She saw her dear Son dying, forsaken, as He yielded up His spirit.*
> *O Mother, fount of love, make me to feel the strength of your grief, so that I may mourn with you!*
> *Make my heart burn with love for Christ, my Lord God, that I may be pleasing to Him!*
> *Holy Mother, this I pray, drive the wounds of the Crucified deep into my heart.*
> *Share with me the pains of your wounded Son who is so gracious to suffer for my sake.*

*Make me truly weep with you, and share the suffering of the Crucified,
     as long as I shall live,*
To stand with you beside the Cross and share your grief is my desire.
*O Virgin, most exalted among virgins, be not bitter toward me; let me
     weep with you!*
*Let me bear the death of Christ, be a sharer of his Passion, contemplate
     His wounds!*
*Let me suffer His pain, let me be engulfed by the Cross, for the love of
     your Son.*
*Lest by devouring flames I be destroyed, Virgin, by you I may be
     defended at the day of judgment.*
*Grant that I may be protected by the Cross, fortified by the death of
     Christ, strengthened by grace.*
*When my body dies, may my soul be granted the glory of paradise.
     Amen.[1]*

CROSS TRAINING

Meditation on the crucifixion and death of Jesus has been at the center of Christian piety for centuries. It has touched the imaginations of many writers, composers, and artists—one can see the history of art by looking at just the way it has been depicted over time. This attention to the cross is very telling: Christians believe that the use of different means can help them to more fully immerse themselves in Christ's life. The stations of the cross, which are artistic representations of the Passion story, appear in many churches. Fasting and various kinds of physical reminders also help many people to remind themselves of the story of Jesus and can enable them to carry an awareness of the stories throughout the day. At different times over history, though, some of these reminders became misguided: some people began to assume that the more they inflicted suffering on themselves, the more they could come to know the sufferings of Christ. Today most people are much less likely to go to these extremes.

There is a kernel of truth, though, in the attempt to make meditation on the passion of Christ a regular part of life. During the third workout, it may be helpful to fast or to give up something, if it helps us to focus on the story of Christ. Experiencing physical hunger, as long as it does not threaten our health, can remind us of our deeper spiritual hunger and thus make us more aware of our dependence on God. In solidarity with the poor, for example, we might for a period of time give up one meal in order to give the money usually spent on it to those who are hungry. This and similar choices will help us to bring the third workout into our everyday life.

SUMMARY OF THE THIRD WORKOUT

The third workout is about walking with Jesus and coming to better understand his final days. We choose to immerse ourselves in his last days, bringing our imagination and our whole lives into contemplation of his death for our sakes. We ask God for the grace to be with Jesus in his suffering, even knowing that we, too, will suffer. Because of this, it is good to be reminded of our foundation: we should seek neither health nor sickness, neither a long life nor a short one; we should seek only to do what Jesus did, namely, to fulfill God's will for us.

In choosing to be with Jesus, we have suffered with him, in the hope that God's will might be fulfilled. As we enter into the fourth workout, then, let us look forward to its completion.

EXERCISES IN THE THIRD WORKOUT

Each scriptural text corresponds to a day's prayer, perhaps even several days' prayer. It will be helpful to return to that text at various points during the day or week and even to condense the text into a word or phrase that will be easy to remember. Again, consider ways in which you might bring your imagination to bear on the themes of these workouts: fasting, giving money to the poor, giving up for a time something you value. Anything that will help you to maintain a focus on the stories of Jesus will help you to more closely identify with him. As always, use the seven practices as you pray, using these texts described in the chapter:

1. Jesus washing the feet of the disciples (Jn 13:3–15)
2. Jesus confronting Judas; the Last Supper (Mt 26:20–30)
3. Jesus in the Garden of Gethsemane (Mt 26:36–46)
4. The arrest of Jesus (Mt 26:47–56)
5. Jesus before the Sanhedrin (Mt 26:57–68)
6. Peter's denial of Jesus (Mt 26:69–75)
7. Jesus before Pontius Pilate (Mt 27:11–23)
8. Jesus being crowned with thorns (Mt 27:27–31)
9. Jesus' crucifixion (Mt 27:35–46)
10. Jesus' death (Lk 23:32–46)
11. Jesus entrusting Mary to John the disciple (Jn 19:25–27)
12. Mary beneath the cross (the *Stabat Mater*)

chapter

fourth workout: sharing Christ's glory

AT THE BEGINNING OF THE THIRD WORKOUT, WE LOOKED AT HOW THERE IS A fundamental paradox in the choice to love another person: love involves sacrifice, the holy offering of a part of oneself. Now, at the beginning of the fourth and final workout, we confront the implications of this paradox: by choosing to love Jesus and to suffer with him, we now share in his triumph over death. In dying with Christ, we now share in his resurrection. St. Paul wrote:

For if we have been united with him in a death like his, we shall certainly be united with him in a resurrection like his. We know

that our old self was crucified with him so that the sinful body
might be destroyed, and we might no longer be enslaved to sin.
For he who has died is freed from sin. But if we have died with
Christ, we believe that we shall also live with him. For we know
that Christ being raised from the dead will never die again;
death no longer has dominion over him. The death he died he
died to sin, once for all, but the life he lives he lives to God.
(Rom 6:5–10)

This is a mystery that the earliest Christians wrestled with: Jesus died a scandalous death, humiliated by his enemies. Yet his death proved to turn their notion of death itself upside down; death became the passage to life. Instead of seeing Jesus as a pitiful wretch overcome by his enemies, they began to see him as an obedient servant of the Father who chose to die in order that others might choose to live. For by showing his disciples that they need not fear death, they were freed to embrace life without fear.

Consider this for a moment: how would your life be different if you knew that you would never die? Now, imagine that you are seeing people around you dying of a highly contagious disease, though you yourself are not yet sick. If you were afraid of death, most likely you would try to get away. But if you did not fear death at all, you would be more likely to take care of the people around you, especially if they were your loved ones. Having no fear of death, in short, would enable you to love others more freely.

This is precisely what happened to the early Christians. Freed from the fear of death, they were able to give themselves to loving others, even under persecution and the threat of execution. Jesus opened for them a whole new dimension of living, based on the promise that they would share in his resurrected life. They were able to choose the path of suffering with the knowledge that their sacrifices were not in vain. Today things have not changed. Not long ago, communities of religious women in China commented on their work with the people in the grip of the deadly SARS epidemic. The *Hong Kong Sunday Examiner* reported on a group of nuns in Hebei Province who, even though the infection rate among health-care workers was high, indicated that their faith made them willing to take the risk and sacrifice themselves for the sake of others.[1]

Resurrection is about God's gift of freedom, the achievement of the fundamental yearning of the human heart. As a prelude to our meditations on the Resurrection, let us call to mind for a moment the things that make us feel unfree. How do you feel tied down? In what ways are you unable to be your truest self? What are the factors in your life that prevent you from achieving happiness? Think about some of the basics: money, relationships with family, jobs or school, commitments of various sorts. In our frenzied lives, we tend to be driven in many ways. We are overworked and have little time to really relax. There's always something else to do, something else to achieve, some other desire that seems to be just outside our grasp, and so we fall into the trap of constantly living in the future. Why? What would it be like to be freed from these stresses, to truly live in the present moment without fear?

Last summer, my family and I spent some time visiting friends who live near a beach. Their son and our daughter are about the same age, and they have a great time together playing in the sand. It is remarkable to watch them. Like many kids, they like digging holes and trenches and constructing elaborate sandcastles. One will be working on a moat, while the other will run down with a pail to scoop the water that will fill it. Their minds are keenly tuned in to this activity—they seem completely engrossed. When I see this, I wonder what they are thinking. Is it even possible that they have any consciousness of their own mortality? Or is it, as I'm more inclined to believe, that their play in the sand represents, during that time, the entirety of creation to them? They are not thinking about what bills need to be paid, what school will be like when they get back, what jobs they will hold when they get older. They are unconcerned about how they look, what others think of them, who hurt them recently. They do not hold on to anxiety, or fear, or negative memories: they are simply alive, imitating God's work of creation.

I wish I could return to that feeling of freedom, of lack of self-consciousness. I think of the image of these children at the beach when I think about Jesus' counsel that we must be like children if we are to enter the kingdom of heaven. Children at play are free; perhaps that is why play is the fundamental aim of childhood. Perhaps too that is why play is still important to us as adults. So much of what we do is a means toward some other end: we go to school to get a job; work to earn money; do chores to keep our homes clean. Play is an end in itself; it is an expression of spontaneous living in the moment. It is possible only when we allow ourselves to step out of the normal flow of our everyday lives and simply be alive.

Our meditations in the fourth workout move us in this direction, because dwelling on the Resurrection helps us overcome the fear of death. Through the lens of the Resurrection, life is not bounded by death—and thus we achieve our freedom in no longer being afraid of it. For while all of us will die one day, our understanding of death changes because of the Resurrection: death becomes little more than the closing of one chapter of our lives and the beginning of another. The resurrected Jesus was almost nonchalant about his own death—extraordinary, since we might expect that someone in his situation could come back to wreak havoc on the political establishment that executed him. Why didn't he hunt down his enemies? Why didn't he use his return from the dead as a platform to call attention to his own power?

Perhaps the reason is because Jesus was truly free. He was not concerned about the pettiness of so much social and political action; he was alive and wanted to bring good news to his friends. He simply wanted to share the joy of being alive. Perhaps too he was more concerned with inviting his friends to share that joy.

In the room where the disciples gathered, an interesting exchange takes place:

*On the evening of that day, the first day of the week, the doors being
shut where the disciples were, for fear of the Jews, Jesus came and
stood among them and said to them, "Peace be with you." When he
had said this, he showed them his hands and his side. Then the disciples were glad when they saw the Lord. Jesus said to them again,
"Peace be with you. As the Father has sent me, even so I send you."
And when he had said this, he breathed on them, and said to them,
"Receive the Holy Spirit. If you forgive the sins of any, they are forgiven; if you retain the sins of any, they are retained." Now Thomas,
one of the twelve, called the Twin, was not with them when Jesus
came. So the other disciples told him, "We have seen the Lord." But
he said to them, "Unless I see in his hands the print of the nails,
and place my finger in the mark of the nails, and place my hand in
his side, I will not believe." Eight days later, his disciples were again
in the house, and Thomas was with them. The doors were shut, but
Jesus came and stood among them, and said, "Peace be with you."
Then he said to Thomas, "Put your finger here, and see my hands;
and put out your hand, and place it in my side; do not be faithless,
but believing." Thomas answered him, "My Lord and my God!"
Jesus said to him, "Have you believed because you have seen me?
Blessed are those who have not seen and yet believe." (Jn 20:19–29)*

Notice that the risen Jesus still bears his wounds. How can it be otherwise? In our own lives, times of suffering may lead to times of peace
and joy, but we cannot escape the lingering effects of suffering. It per-
manently changes us—we cannot pretend that it never happened.
That the risen Jesus still bears his wounds is good news, for it tells us
that there is a continuity between the lives we have now and the lives
that we will enjoy in the Resurrection. Jesus is the same person. His
wounds, though, are different: they are not a source of suffering but a
source of recognition. It is only through seeing Jesus' wounds that
Thomas recognizes him. In the Resurrection, we will still bear the
effects of the hurts that have been done to us, but they will no longer
cause us pain.

The fourth workout is about celebrating the new life of Jesus and the new life that we can anticipate by our choice to live with Jesus. It begins with meditations on the stories of Jesus' resurrection and culminates with the contemplation on love. Read through the chapter, then begin with several days' prayer on the Resurrection stories. Then spend several days on the contemplation on love.

THE RESURRECTION

Earlier I cited lines from John Donne's famous sonnet "Death, Be Not Proud." Here is the rest of the text, which stands as a meditation on this Christian view of death, in light of Christ's resurrection:

> *Death, be not proud, though some have called thee*
> *Mighty and dreadful, for thou art not so;*
> *For those whom thou think'st thou dost overthrow,*
> *Die not, poor Death, nor yet canst thou kill me.*
> *From rest and sleep, which but thy pictures be,*
> *Much pleasure; then from thee much more must flow,*
> *And soonest our best men with thee do go,*
> *Rest of their bones, and soul's delivery.*
> *Thou art slave to fate, chance, kings, and desperate men,*
> *And dost with poison, war, and sickness dwell;*
> *And poppy or charms can make us sleep as well*
> *And better than thy stroke; why swell'st thou then?*
> *One short sleep past, we wake eternally,*
> *And death shall be no more; Death, thou shalt die.*

To suffer with Jesus is to share in Jesus' joy in the Resurrection. Jesus has put death to death, such that what remains is only the fullness of life with God. The fourth workout, then, is about joy. While we tried to focus on the somber mood during the third workout, now our mood is of happiness, excitement, hopefulness. The third workout was the slow toll of bells during a funeral procession; the fourth workout is the ebullient peals of the cathedral on Easter morning. Orthodox Christians celebrate Easter with the exclamations "Christ is risen!" and "He is truly risen!" Alleluia.

The Empty Tomb

And when the sabbath was past, Mary Magdalene, and Mary the mother of James, and Salome, bought spices, so that they might go and anoint him. And very early on the first day of the week they went to the tomb when the sun had risen. And they were saying to one another, "Who will roll away the stone for us from the door of the tomb?" And looking up, they saw that the stone was rolled back;—it was very large. And entering the tomb, they saw a young man sitting on the right side, dressed in a white robe; and they were amazed. And he said to them, "Do not be amazed; you seek Jesus of Nazareth, who was crucified. He has risen, he is not here; see the place where they laid him. But go, tell his disciples and Peter that he is going before you to Galilee; there you will see him, as he told you." And they went out and fled from the tomb; for trembling and astonishment had come upon them; and they said nothing to any one, for they were afraid. (Mk 16:1–8)

As you imagine this story, feel in your body the fear, amazement, and anticipation that Mary Magdalene, Mary the mother of James, and Salome felt. Allow yourself to pay attention to the breathlessness they feel: they have come in mourning but leave with the hope against all hope that the one they love is alive again! How do you react?

Appearance to Mary Magdalene

But Mary stood weeping outside the tomb, and as she wept she stooped to look into the tomb; and she saw two angels in white, sitting where the body of Jesus had lain, one at the head and one at

*the feet. They said to her, "Woman, why are you weeping?" She said
to them, "Because they have taken away my Lord, and I do not
know where they have laid him." Saying this, she turned round and
saw Jesus standing, but she did not know that it was Jesus. Jesus
said to her, "Woman, why are you weeping? Whom do you seek?"
Supposing him to be the gardener, she said to him, "Sir, if you have
carried him away, tell me where you have laid him, and I will take
him away." Jesus said to her, "Mary." She turned and said to him
in Hebrew, "Rabbouni!" (which means Teacher). Jesus said to her,
"Do not hold me, for I have not yet ascended to the Father; but go
to my brethren and say to them, I am ascending to my Father and
your Father, to my God and your God." Mary Magdalene went and
said to the disciples, "I have seen the Lord"; and she told them that
he had said these things to her. (Jn 20:11–18)*

Mary of Magdala is blessed indeed: she is the first to speak to the risen
Jesus. How does she feel when she utters, "Rabbouni!"? What is going
through her mind? Her heart? What does she want to say to him,
even though she is too dumbfounded to find the words? What would
you want to say if you were in her place?

Emmaus

*That very day two of them were going to a village named Emmaus,
about seven miles from Jerusalem, and talking with each other
about all these things that had happened. While they were talking
and discussing together, Jesus himself drew near and went with
them. But their eyes were kept from recognizing him. And he said
to them, "What is this conversation which you are holding with
each other as you walk?" And they stood still, looking sad. Then
one of them, named Cleopas, answered him, "Are you the only visi-
tor to Jerusalem who does not know the things that have happened
there in these days?" And he said to them, "What things?" And they
said to him, "Concerning Jesus of Nazareth, who was a prophet*

*mighty in deed and word before God and all the people, and how
our chief priests and rulers delivered him up to be condemned to
death, and crucified him. But we had hoped that he was the one to
redeem Israel. Yes, and besides all this, it is now the third day since
this happened. Moreover, some women of our company amazed us.
They were at the tomb early in the morning and did not find his
body; and they came back saying that they had even seen a vision
of angels, who said that he was alive. Some of those who were with
us went to the tomb, and found it just as the women had said; but
him they did not see." And he said to them, "O foolish men, and
slow of heart to believe all that the prophets have spoken! Was it
not necessary that the Christ should suffer these things and enter
into his glory?" And beginning with Moses and all the prophets, he
interpreted to them in all the scriptures the things concerning himself. So they drew near to the village to which they were going. He
appeared to be going further, but they constrained him, saying,
"Stay with us, for it is toward evening and the day is now far
spent." So he went in to stay with them. When he was at table
with them, he took the bread and blessed, and broke it, and gave it
to them. And their eyes were opened and they recognized him; and
he vanished out of their sight. They said to each other, "Did not
our hearts burn within us while he talked to us on the road, while
he opened to us the scriptures?" (Lk 24:13–32)*

The disciples on the road to Emmaus are caught up in the story of
Jesus' resurrection, which has circulated among his followers. Like so
many others, they are confused and excited at what this means.
Perhaps it is their incredulity that keeps them from recognizing
Jesus—perhaps they expected him to be different, like a ghost.

What do you expect the risen Jesus to be like? Perhaps there are
ways that our expectations of Jesus hinder us from recognizing him as
well. Perhaps he is here among us, as he was with the disciples on the
road to Emmaus, but we, too, fail to recognize him. It is very telling
that they finally do recognize him in the breaking of the bread: the
repetition of this ritual action opens their eyes to see him as he really is.

The question the disciples pose at the end of the story is striking: "Did not our hearts burn within us?" This question points to why it is important to pay attention to our own emotions in prayer. Jesus walks with the disciples for a long time before they know it is he; perhaps if they had been more attentive to their own hearts, they would have recognized him sooner. Perhaps we, too, might more quickly recognize Jesus, and share in his joy, by paying attention to what moves us.

Commissioning the Disciples

Now the eleven disciples went to Galilee, to the mountain to which Jesus had directed them. And when they saw him they worshiped him; but some doubted. And Jesus came and said to them, "All authority in heaven and on earth has been given to me. Go therefore and make disciples of all nations, baptizing them in the name of the Father and of the Son and of the Holy Spirit, teaching them to observe all that I have commanded you; and lo, I am with you always, to the close of the age." (Mt 28:16–20)

Jesus' final words to his disciples are hopeful and promising. He tells them to spread the Good News and assures them that he is with them always. In light of the Emmaus story, it is good to remember these words. There will be times in our lives when Jesus seems absent; these words suggest that such experiences have more to do with our false expectations than they have to do with Jesus. "I am with you always." Unlike the disciples, who were afraid and ran away when Jesus was arrested, Jesus promises never to leave us. He promises to love us always; let us turn to contemplate how we can love him in return.

CONTEMPLATION ON LOVE

At the end of his book, Ignatius writes that "we should value above everything else the great service which is given to God because of pure love."[2] For him, love was the proper response of the human being in gratefulness to God for creation itself. This love, he held, was manifested not only in emotion or pious language but in the kinds of choices people make by their living. A lover gives to the beloved what he or she has; and in return, the beloved does the same.

The contemplation on love is about envisioning how we choose to love the God who loves us. If God is the divine lover, we as the beloved must look at what God has given us in order that we may freely offer it back to God. Recall the parable of the talents: the good servant is the one who takes what the master has given, cultivates it, and gives it back to the master.

Begin by picturing yourself in God's presence. Ask God to give you awareness of all the gifts God has given you over the course of your life, and ask further for a spirit of gratitude. As you pay attention to these gifts, consider the ways that you might use them for God's greater glory and how you might offer them back to God. Give thanks for

Creation itself
Your ancestors and those who struggled to give you life
Your biological mother and father, whether you know them or
   not
Your immediate family, whether related by blood or not
Your body, whether you like the way it is or not
Your faculties of sense, even if some seem faulty
Your intelligence, whether or not you think you have enough
   of it
Your special talents, whether or not you think them useful
Your friends and loved ones, whether alive or dead
Your work, whether for money or not
Your play, even though it may seem infrequent
Your possessions, no matter how much money they are worth
Your time to live, no matter how quickly it seems to pass

Keep in mind a firm purpose to take this contemplation into everyday life. As we near the end of the spiritual workouts, we must begin to look ahead to how we might apply them. Life involves so many challenges; by paying attention to the ways that God has gifted us, we can begin to appreciate the ways our gifts enable us to live more fully.

Great athletes love challenges. While watching the Olympics recently, I was struck by how many athletes talked about wanting to break a world record or beat a particular opponent. Instead of seeing these challenges as roadblocks to their own comfort and ease, they saw them as opportunities to let their gifts manifest themselves. Often, these athletes had to face great hurdles; many did not accomplish what they had hoped. But they were grateful for the chance. I often wish that I could bring a similar drive into ordinary life, with the ability to see challenges as ways to manifest the gifts God has given me. But the truth is that, more often, I see them as unnecessary hassles and often blame God for them.

Focus on seeing yourself with the same thrill that God has when looking at you. Consider yourself one of God's great works of art, one that God earnestly hopes will choose to love God freely as God loves you. Consider the words of Ignatius, resolving to offer back to God what God has given you. Impress this prayer on your heart and mind; write it down and put it in your wallet or purse, and look at it often. Make this prayer part of your way of looking at the world:

Take, Lord, and receive all my liberty, my memory, my understanding, and all my will—all that I have and possess. You, Lord, have given all that to me. I now give it back to you, O Lord. All of it is yours. Dispose of it according to your will. Give me your love and your grace, for that is enough for me.[3]

This contemplation on love can help us develop a greater viewpoint toward our daily lives so that we might focus less on the difficulty of whatever challenges we face and more on the gifts God gives us to face them. The goal is to see the world not as some kind of testing ground but, rather, as a place "charged with the grandeur of God," where God's gifts are omnipresent. As we continue in this contemplation, then, we focus on the world around us, where God's artistry is spread like "heaven's embroidered cloths," to use a phrase from Yeats.

Let us thank God for the beauty of the world around us: the stars at night; the air we breathe; the change of seasons; the spontaneous movements of flowers blooming and trees growing; the smell of coming rain; the warmth of sun on our faces; the sound of crashing waves; the serenity of falling snow; the majesty of mountaintops; the mystery of oceans; the beauty of forests; the placidity of beaches; the basic goodness of the freshly cut grass at the park.

Let us thank God for all the creatures in the world, both large and small, those that we see and those that we don't; for the delicate and profound system of interrelatedness of which we human beings are a part; for the vastness of the ecosystem (and the necessity to preserve it); for the ways that other creatures contribute to our wellbeing by what they do; for the sublime truths that we sometimes apprehend about ourselves by paying attention to other creatures; for our own creatureliness and our dependence on so great a God, who is more capable than we of understanding the world and our roles in it.

Let us again thank God for ourselves, keeping in mind the ways that God has bestowed on us gifts that surpass the other gifts in the created order: divine likeness. God has given us not only the biological beauty of cells, organs, and tissues; not only the beauty of motion that the animals possess; not only the capacity for intelligence shown in certain animals; God has also given us the ability to seek God and to seek to be like God. Each breath that we take is another gift that God gives us in order that we might seek God. And how we seek God! We seek personal happiness; we seek self-improvement; we seek beauty; we seek power; we seek other people to love and from whom to receive love. And while all of us have often missed the mark in the ways that we seek, still there is within us a drive toward self-transcendence, a drive that culminates, and is perfected, in the love of God.

We thus thank God for what drives us forward in life, toward greater goodness, truth, and beauty. We thank God for giving us the ability to know our own sin so that in knowing it, we might turn away from it toward greater freedom and life. We thank God for the many mercies God shows us even while we are still sinners, welcoming us with open arms like the prodigal father. We thank God for the people who have shown us God's love even when we were unaware of it: people both living and dead whose sainthood, however ephemeral, has helped us to know ourselves better. We thank God, whose motherly love always wishes more for us even when we are content with our limited selves. We thank God for the ability to turn in prayer at all times to the one who knows us better than we know ourselves (Ps 139).

Now we ask God to make our hearts pure so that we might be ready to see opportunities in our experiences to praise, reverence, and serve God. We ask for the grace to love the people in our lives: our families, our friends, our neighbors, our coworkers, our acquaintances, and complete strangers and enemies. We ask for the wisdom to understand the ways our lives must change in order to become more loving, both on a personal and social level. We pray for the grace of contemplative action, that everything we do may arise out of a deep, daily commitment to make our lives, choices, and actions reflect an abiding love for God.

We close with the prayer of Jesus, making his prayer our prayer:

Our father in heaven, may your name be holy always!
May your world be here among us,
So that everyone chooses what you will,
Both in heaven and on earth.
Give us food today,
And forgive us whenever we do wrong,
In the same way that we choose to forgive others.
Do not make us face the final test,
And lead us away from evil.[4]

SUMMARY OF THE FOURTH WORKOUT

The fourth workout is a meditation on the resurrection of Jesus and a request that God help us to live as Jesus did, in perfect love. The five meditations from the Gospels help us to more fully appreciate how the Resurrection changes not only the meaning of Jesus' death but also the very meaning of our lives—we who hope to share in the Resurrection one day. These meditations should help us to focus on the ways that God calls us to greater life, passing through death.

The contemplation on love is the culmination of the spiritual workouts, both because it is the last exercise and because it represents the very goal of the workouts. Describing how to live a virtuous life, St. Augustine once wrote, "Love, and do what you will." The contemplation on love is ultimately the prayer that our lives might become so suffused with the love of God that everything we do might reflect this love in action. To be a spiritually mature person is to be a person who loves in all things. This must be our goal.

EXERCISES IN THE FOURTH WORKOUT

1. Thomas's doubting of Jesus (Jn 20:19–29)
2. The empty tomb (Mk 16:1–8)
3. The appearance to Mary Magdalene (Jn 20:11–18)
4. The road to Emmaus (Lk 24:13–32)
5. The commissioning of the disciples (Mt 28:16–20)
6. The contemplation on love

conclusion

AT THE BEGINNING OF THIS BOOK, WE EXPLORED THE THEME OF WORKING
out as a metaphor for the spiritual life. We will carry this metaphor
one step further and then examine how, like any metaphor, it is
limited.

Athletes who begin a regimen of working out do so because they
hope that it will prepare them for competition. They have a goal in
mind; in short, the workouts are not ends in themselves. After the
contemplation on divine love, it is important to remember that the
spiritual workouts are, in the end, ways to help us become more loving human beings. Prayer is certainly good in itself, inasmuch as it is

about communicating with the God who, as St. Augustine pointed out, created us for God's own self. But there is another dimension to prayer, a dimension that opens us in love toward others. To do the workouts well means to take them into our everyday lives, such that by doing them, we are transformed into persons more capable of loving God by loving those around us.

Let us bring our metaphor to its logical conclusion: the spiritual workout is preparation for the human "race." To be human is to be a spiritual person caught up in an extraordinarily complex world, one in which it is easy to become distracted from the goal: union with God. Bringing these practices into conversation with our everyday lives can help us to retain a certain clarity, a single-mindedness that reminds us to see all things as opportunities to grow in the love of God. But even the practice of spirituality can sidetrack us and become an end in itself. Today many people see spirituality as something that can give them greater happiness, and so they pursue it for its benefits to health and inner peace. These are indeed good by-products of spirituality, but they are not the substance. The substance of the spiritual life, that to which it is ordered, is God: spirituality is the practice of communion with God. In light of this, let us observe some of the ways we must leave behind the metaphor of the workout.

WORKOUTS AND REST

At the heart of the spiritual workout is the opportunity to respond to Jesus' invitation: "Come, follow me." We have explored some ways to respond: that is, ways in which we can take the initiative to *do something*. Let us turn to a complementary metaphor—namely, friendship—which suggests to us an equally important movement in the spiritual life: *resting* in the care of the beloved.

Deep friendships last because each person can rest in the love of the other. At a certain point, it becomes clear that I don't have to do anything to make the other love me; the other chooses to do this because he or she values me. Clearly, friends will freely choose to do nice things for each other: celebrating birthdays, going out, talking on the phone, sharing free time. But none of these things causes the friendship. Real friendship takes on a momentum of its own.

The same is true of our relationship to God. We don't have to *do* anything in order for God to love us. (As a side note, early Christians wrestled against a heretical group called the Pelagians, who held that a person had to earn his or her way into heaven.) God chooses to love us freely, Jesus promises us, and cares for us no matter what we do. In light of this truth, then, we must consider the implications of our taking action in the spiritual life. What do spiritual workouts gain us if God loves us no matter what we do?

Prayer is not for God's sake but for our own. Through prayer, we come to greater awareness of the ways that God is present to us in our everyday lives, and moreover, prayer helps us to develop an awareness of the sacred everywhere. Prayer gives us greater peace and happiness because it is the constant reminder that we are thrust into a world where God is everywhere, if we would only look. This is not to say, by the way, that we pretend there is no suffering. Instead, it is to say that we begin to see suffering differently—no less painful, but still a place where God takes us, weeping (I believe), into a mother's arms. It helps us to trust that suffering is the peculiar, privileged place of encounter with divine love, the place where we are brought like infants into new birth. It helps us to trust that the process of suffering is but a passage, one that may cause us to cry out in despair, and yet to maintain hope that God is on the other side, welcoming us into even greater life.

In short, prayer helps us to pay attention not to what *we are doing* but to what *God is doing* to us, with us, and for us. Ultimately, all we can do is rest in the care of the divine lover.

In my own life, this has been an intensely difficult lesson. Anyone who, like me, has led a mostly carefree youth will find the first experience of real suffering difficult. It feels like God is abandoning us and seems that the world as we knew it is now gone. How easy it can be to deny God when we are suffering! My own reaction was one of sheer confusion: How can this possibly be? The experience of any suffering simply does not fit with our vision of ourselves. This point was clear to me recently when I had to take my eighteen-month-old daughter to the doctor for her immunizations. My wife and I had to hold her down on the table while the injections were administered, and the look on her face was clear: *How can you let this happen to me!* Even on a baby, this look was obvious. She could not understand how people who she thought loved her could allow her to experience that kind of pain and suffering.

The image that began to form in my imagination after a period of some three difficult years was that of a field upon which soft rain begins to fall. In springtime, before seeds begin to sprout, rain must water the fields for the good of the crop. I imagined myself as that field: there was nothing that I could do to hurry along the growth of my own hope. I could only allow God to water the field and allow the growth to happen in due time. This made me impatient; I don't like waiting, and my urge was to do something to hurry it along. But I—couldn't—I had to wait.

The spiritual workout is part of the larger dialogue between ourselves and God. It is a friendship; and like any friendship, it will develop in its own time. There are things we can do to cultivate this friendship, but in the end, we cannot force it. We must allow God to act freely, just as God allows us to act freely.

DISCIPLINE AND FREEDOM

Let us carry the metaphor of friendship one step further by observing that relationships do not follow a precise schedule. The metaphor of the workout suggests, perhaps, that we can plan on definite improvement by disciplined attention. The metaphor of friendship, though, gets us closer to the truth: it is difficult to discern what "improvement" is. Moreover, the goal is not improvement but deepening the friendship with shared experience. While sometimes discipline can help us to pay attention to what we value, in prayer there is a point when we must simply allow God to do whatever God wills for us. We do not set the schedule; God is God, we are creatures. We cannot force God to obey our wills, even though we frequently try.

Ignatius wrote a maxim that applies to this balance between discipline and freedom: "With regard to any project, we must put ourselves in God's hands as if our success depended on Him, but with regard to choosing the means and doing the work, we must labor as if everything depended on us."[1] The challenge is to find the right balance between discipline and freedom, such that one's friendship with God can deepen. Prayer is certainly an important element in this friendship but not the only one. Moreover, some people find that some of their most deeply meaningful moments come not in formal prayer but in everyday action. Perhaps the distinctions we make between prayer and action are too sharp.

Do not have preconceptions about what constitutes prayer. I have learned, after a long time, that I pray best when I am moving. It took me a long time to learn this because my image of prayer involved sitting peacefully with my eyes closed. After many occasions when I fell asleep, I started to wonder. I compared these experiences with times when I've been out for a good row, bike ride, or walk, and realized that those activities have helped me clear my mind and attend to the simple joy of being alive in God's presence. Paradoxically, some of these experiences didn't involve the explicit intention to pray; it just happened spontaneously. I am encouraged by Paul's description of prayer: "The Spirit helps us in our weakness; for we do not know how to pray as we ought, but the Spirit himself intercedes for us with sighs too deep for words" (Rom 8:26). In time, we must all learn that it is not we who are praying but God who is praying because we allow it to happen. The most authentic prayer, then, will not happen when we schedule it. It will happen because we have offered no barriers to the freedom of the Holy Spirit working through us. It will happen at unexpected moments: at work, in conversations, on vacations, while driving, while in pain. We will find, in an instant, that the boundary between our ordinary experience and the sacred is gone.

These moments of clarity happen according to God's timeline, not our own, so we must be prepared for them at any time. Here again is a clue to why we need the spiritual workout: it helps us to drop the barriers that we otherwise keep in place. Today it is easy to live on guard; we construct false selves because we perceive a need to advance whatever causes we take on. We must do better at work; we must find the perfect mate; we must earn respect from others; we must not allow people to take advantage of us. Our false selves are those personas we assume in order to shield our most authentic selves from the hurt of others. Sadly, though, we often forget that these personas are only masks and that we must put them aside in order for our authentic selves to grow. The spiritual workout helps us to pay attention to our authentic selves, for they are the sacred space of encounter with God. And over time, by cultivating these authentic selves, we find that we can more readily respond to the ways that God touches us there when we least expect it.

I close with a hopeful observation. There is a freshness in learning to pray; and the good news is that we are always learning. I am moved by the comment of Zen master Shunryu Suzuki, who in describing the practice of *zazen* (sitting) said that one must have the "beginner's mind," the attitude that one is doing it for the first time.[2] The most authentic practitioner of Zen, in other words, is the one who does it for the first time, for he or she brings no preconceptions. So too it is in our prayer with God: we must treat it as something new, no matter how long we have been learning. If you feel like you are going nowhere, do not despair; you are not alone. I have been trying to learn how to pray for years now; and as new life stages happen, I feel like I'm starting all over again, like a confused child. By now, though, I am a little less afraid of that confusion than I once was. I am perhaps a little more willing to tolerate the feeling of going nowhere, and I am working hard to learn patience (what else can I do?). The image that sticks in my mind is that of Moses on Mount Sinai. He asks to see God, and God's reply is that God's glory is too great to be seen directly; Moses will only be allowed to see God from behind as God passes by. I like the image of seeing God from behind: for I, like many others, recognize the work of God in my life most clearly in retrospect. My prayer is that after practicing the Ignatian workout, you too will look back and see God passing by.

notes

INTRODUCTION

1. Ignatius of Loyola, "Autobiography," in *Ignatius of Loyola: The Spiritual Exercises and Selected Works,* ed. George E. Ganss (New York: Paulist Press, 1991), 68. Hereafter this volume will be referred to as simply "Ganss."

2. Ibid., 71.

3. Ibid.

4. My paraphrase of Ignatius of Loyola, *Spiritual Exercises* 23, based on Ganss, 130.

1. WHAT TO EXPECT IN SPIRITUAL WORKOUTS

1. Gerard W. Hughes, *God of Surprises* (London: Darton, Longman and Todd, 1985).

2. My paraphrase of Ignatius of Loyola, *Spiritual Exercises* 1, in Ganss, 121.

2. TWO BEGINNING EXERCISES

1. St. Augustine, *Confessions: A New Translation by Rex Warner,* trans. Rex Warner (New York: New American Library, 1963), X, 3, 211–12.

2. For these suggestions on the daily examen, I rely on Dennis Hamm, "Rummaging for God: Praying backward through Your Day," *America,* 14 May 1994, 22–23.

3. Some of this material is influenced by the examen in Joseph A. Tetlow, *Choosing Christ in the World: Directing the Spiritual Exercises of St. Ignatius Loyola according to Annotations Eighteen and Nineteen: A Handbook* (St. Louis: Institute of Jesuit Sources, 1989).

3. HOW TO GET THE MOST OUT OF YOUR WORKOUTS

1. This translation is by Seamus Heaney, in *Dante's Inferno: Translations by Twenty Contemporary Poets,* ed. Daniel Halpern (Hopewell, N.J.: Ecco Press, 1993), 3.

4. THE FOUNDATION

1. St. Augustine, *Confessions* I,1, my paraphrase.

6. SECOND WORKOUT

1. My paraphrase of selections taken from Ignatius of Loyola, "The Deliberation on Poverty," in Ganss, 225–26. I have edited the section titles for the sake of clarity.

2. Fyodor Dostoyevsky, *The Brothers Karamazov,* trans. Constance Garnett (New York: Modern Library), 378.

3. John Donne, "Death, be not proud," originally published in *Poems, by J.D. With elegies on the authors death* (1633). An online version can be found in the University of Toronto's Representative Poetry Online site (http://eir.library.utoronto.ca/rpo/display/poem658.html), copyright 2003.

7. THIRD WORKOUT

1. This translation is my own. I have compared it with a number of extant translations for the sake of accuracy.

8. FOURTH WORKOUT

1. "Sisters volunteer to serve SARS patients in Hebei" in *Hong Kong Sunday Examiner,* 1 June 2003, 3.

2. Ignatius of Loyola, *The Spiritual Exercises* 370 in Ganss, 213

3. Ignatius of Loyola, *The Spiritual Exercises* 234 in Ganss, 177.

4. This is my paraphrase of the Lord's Prayer, based on the text in Matthew 6:9–14.

CONCLUSION

1. This saying attributed to Ignatius is found in D. Bartoli, *Histoire de Saint Ignace et de l'origine de la Compagnie de Jésus,* 3rd ed., 2 v. (Brussels, 1852), 2: 254. Translation of the original Italian of 1650.

2. Shunryu Suzuki, *Zen Mind, Beginner's Mind* (New York: Weatherhill, 1997).

books and web sites for further reading

BOOKS

Albom, Mitch. *Tuesdays with Morrie: An Old Man, a Young Man, and Life's Greatest Lesson.* New York: Doubleday, 1997.
A beautiful true story of a writer's ongoing conversations and life lessons with his former professor, who is slowly dying of Lou Gehrig's disease. It is a moving example of how openness to one's terminal illness can produce spiritual fruit.

Augustine, St. *Confessions.* (Several English translations available.)
A sometimes difficult book to read but worthwhile. Augustine's spiritual autobiography moves from self-reflection to prayer to theological musing, sometimes in a single paragraph, and is thus not for everyone. But those of a more intellectual bent may enjoy hearing the stories of a fifth-century saint whose life was about many of the same struggles young adults face today.

Barry, William A. *Letting God Come Close: An Approach to the Ignatian Spiritual Exercises.* Chicago: Jesuit Way, 2001.
"Having served as a spiritual director for more than thirty years, Fr. William Barry has honed his approach to directing the Exercises, an approach that is considered imaginative, innovative, and yet faithful to the intent of Ignatius. He uses clear, down-to-earth examples from his own experience to instill in the director the trust, confidence, and

skills he or she needs to help the retreatant approach God" (from the publisher).

Bellafiore, I. Michael, and Michael Sparough. *Ignatius Loyola: The Story of the Pilgrim*. Chicago: Loyola Press. Video.
The saint's story is portrayed in this one-man dramatization.

Bernardin, Joseph. *The Gift of Peace: Personal Reflections*. Chicago: Loyola Press, 1997.
The spiritual autobiography of the former cardinal archbishop of Chicago in the last years of his life as he meditated on his struggles with unjust accusations and the suffering brought about by his eventually terminal cancer.

English, John J. *Spiritual Freedom: From an Experience of the Ignatian Exercises to the Art of Spiritual Guidance*. 2nd ed. Chicago: Loyola University Press, 1995.
"This new edition of Fr. English's classic text expands his original work to include a new preface, a more comprehensive bibliography, and three additional chapters. Using his own experience as a spiritual guide, Fr. English leads the readers through the meditations of the Spiritual Exercises and provides spiritual counselors with a deeper understanding of the fundamental principles in the Exercises" (from the publisher).

Hughes, Gerard W. *God of Surprises*. London: Darton, Longman and Todd, 1985.
One of the best, most accessible works in spirituality in the last couple of decades, written by an author whose many works are motivated by Ignatian spirituality. It is suitable for young adults and those who are beginners on the spiritual journey.

Ignatius of Loyola. "Spiritual Exercises." In *Ignatius of Loyola: The Spiritual Exercises and Selected Works*. Edited by George E. Ganss. New York: Paulist Press, 1991.

The original texts written by the pen of Ignatius are collected in this scholarly work, amply annotated. This book is for those wishing to do further academic study of St. Ignatius.

Link, Mark. *Vision 2000: Praying Scripture in a Contemporary Way.*
    Allen, Tex.: Tabor Publishing, 1992.
A day-by-day series of meditations using the lectionary readings. They are short and very readable, good for people with busy lives.

Mariani, Paul. *Thirty Days: On Retreat with the Exercises of St. Ignatius.*
    New York: Viking, 2002.
A poet's journal of his own thirty-day retreat.

Martin, James. *In Good Company: The Fast Track from the Corporate
    World to Poverty, Chastity, and Obedience.* Franklin, Wis.: Sheed &
    Ward, 2000.
The spiritual autobiography of a man who left corporate America to become a Jesuit. His straightforward language makes you wonder why everyone doesn't leave corporate America to answer the desires of the heart.

Merton, Thomas. *The Seven Storey Mountain.* New York: Harcourt,
    Brace, 1948.
The spiritual autobiography of a man whose young life as an atheist slowly developed, during his days at Columbia University, toward his conversion to Christianity and eventual acceptance of monastic life. Merton is perhaps the most well known writer on Christian spirituality from the twentieth century.

Ravier, André. *A Do-It-at-Home Retreat: The Spiritual Exercises of
    St. Ignatius of Loyola according to the "Nineteenth Annotation."*
    Translated by Cornelius Michael Buckley. San Francisco: Ignatius
    Press, 1991.
A useful book for individuals and groups seeking to integrate Ignatius's *Spiritual Exercises* into a structured retreat in daily life.

It follows the structure of Ignatius's work very closely and thus is perhaps most appropriate for those who already have some understanding of the work.

Silf, Margaret. *Inner Compass: An Invitation to Ignatian Spirituality.*
  Chicago: Jesuit Way, 1999.
A thoughtful, accessible beginner's guide to Ignatian spirituality written by a British laywoman. It emphasizes this spirituality as a way to pay attention to the inner life and will be useful for adults looking for a writer who speaks from her own experience of practicing Ignatian spirituality.

Smith, Carol Ann, and Eugene F. Merz. *Moment by Moment: A Retreat in Everyday Life.* Notre Dame, Ind.: Ave Maria Press, 2000.
A beautifully illustrated meditative guide to integrating prayer into everyday life. In a series of thirty-two "moments," the text guides the reader with thought-provoking questions, practical suggestions, and excerpts carefully chosen from Scripture and the *Spiritual Exercises.*

Tetlow, Joseph A. *Ignatius Loyola: Spiritual Exercises.* New York: Crossroad, 1996.
A very readable introduction and commentary on the text of the *Spiritual Exercises* by a distinguished scholar and director in the field of Ignatian spirituality.

Willig, Jim, with Tammy Bundy. *Lessons from the School of Suffering: A Young Priest with Cancer Teaches Us How to Live.* Cincinnati, Ohio: St. Anthony Messenger Press, 2001.
Fr. Jim reflects on how Ignatian spirituality helps him to confront the reality of his own cancer and eventual death.

WEB SITES

There are many Web sites on the subject of Ignatian spirituality. Of note are the many centers for Ignatian spirituality on the campuses of Jesuit colleges and universities around the world. Many offer programs not only to students but to the public as well. Listed below, however, are those sites that are of more general interest. (Please note that sometimes Web sites change; those listed here are valid as of the writing of this book.)

http://www.jesuit.org
A gateway to all things related to Ignatian spirituality, sponsored by the Society of Jesus in the United States. Includes links to Jesuit retreat houses around the world, the full text of the *Spiritual Exercises,* suggestions for integrating prayer into daily life, and an extensive bibliography.

http://www.creighton.edu/CollaborativeMinistry/cmo-retreat.html
This site, sponsored by Creighton University's Collaborative Ministry Office, offers an online retreat using the *Spiritual Exercises.*

http://www.creighton.edu/CollaborativeMinistry/daily.html
Also from the Creighton University Collaborative Ministry Office, this calendar links to a reflection for each day, based on daily readings. The reflections are written by various members of the Creighton faculty, staff, and administration. (Includes instructions for converting the reflections for inclusion on a palm PC or personal digital assistant.)

http://www.nwjesuits.org/dailyw/index.htm
A self-guided retreat with daily reflections, excerpts from the *Spiritual Exercises,* and Scripture passages, organized over thirty-seven weeks. From the Oregon Province of the Society of Jesus.

http://www.usccb.org/nab/index.htm
The readings for each day's liturgy from the New American Bible on the Web site of the United States Conference of Catholic Bishops.

http://v2000.org/index.htm
Scriptural reflections for each day, taken from the Vision 2000 series by Mark Link, S.J.

http://goajesuits.org/prayers/praying.htm
A collection of prayers and methods of prayer from the Jesuits in the Goa province on the western coast of India.

http://www.creighton.edu/CLC-NorthCentral/
The home page of the Christian Life Community movement, a lay organization based on the practice of Ignatian spirituality.

http://www.sacredspace.ie
The Irish Jesuits have put together a very user-friendly daily prayer guide based on the *Spiritual Exercises.* The guide is available in many languages.

retreat houses in the united states and canada

The following is a list of retreat centers that offer retreats and spiritual direction in the tradition of the *Spiritual Exercises*. There are many other good retreat houses not specifically oriented around Ignatian spirituality; these can be located either on the Web or by contacting local Catholic dioceses. A more extensive list of Jesuit retreat centers around the world can be found at http://www.jesuit.org. Please note that sometimes Web pages and e-mail addresses change.

UNITED STATES

ALASKA

Holy Spirit Center
10980 Hillside Drive
Anchorage, AK 99507
phone: (907) 346-2343
e-mail: hsrh@alaska.com
Web site: http://home.gci.net/~hsrh/

CALIFORNIA

El Retiro San Iñigo Jesuit Retreat House
300 Manresa Way
Los Altos, CA 94022
phone: (650) 948-4491
fax: (650) 948-0640
e-mail: retreat@elretiro.org
Web site: http://www.elretiro.org

Loyola Institute for Spirituality
480 S Batavia Street
Orange, CA 92868-3907
phone: (714) 997-9587
fax: (714) 997-9588
e-mail: loyinst@pacbell.net
Web site: http://www.loyolainstitute.org/cgi-bin/template.pl?
content=home.shtml

Spiritual Ministry Center
4822 Del Mar Avenue
San Diego, CA 92107
phone: (619) 224-9444
fax: (619) 224-1082
e-mail: SPIRITMIN@aol.com

COLORADO

Sacred Heart Jesuit Retreat House
4801 N Highway 67
P.O. Box 185
Sedalia, CO 80135
phone: (303) 688-4198 ext. 100
e-mail: shjesrh@aol.com
Web site: http://www.sacredheartretreat.org/about.html

FLORIDA

Cenacle Spiritual Life Center
1400 S Dixie Highway
Lantana, FL 33462-5492
phone: (561) 582-2534
fax: (561) 582-8070
e-mail: CenacleFL@aol.com
Web site: http://www.cenaclesisters.org

Manresa Retreat House
12190 SW 56 Street (Miller Drive)
P.O. Box 651512
Miami, FL 33165
phone: (305) 596-0001
fax: (305) 596-9655
e-mail: manresa@bellsouth.net
Web site: http://www.efjc.com/

GEORGIA

Ignatius House Retreat Center
6700 Riverside Drive NW
Atlanta, GA 30328
phone: (404) 255-0503
fax: (404) 256-0776
e-mail: angelret@bellsouth.net
Web site: http://www.ignatiushouse.org/

ILLINOIS

Bellarmine Jesuit Retreat House
175 W County Line Road
Barrington, IL 60011-4043
phone: (847) 381-1261
fax: (847) 381-4695
e-mail: Bellarmine_Jesuits@hotmail.com
Web site: http://www.jesuits-chi.org/retreat/bellarmine.htm

IOWA

Creighton University Retreat Center
16493 Contrail Avenue
Griswold, IA 51535-9406
phone: (712) 778-2466
fax: (712) 778-2467
e-mail: curc@netins.net
Web site: http://www.creighton.edu/CURC/curc.html

LOUISIANA

Jesuit Spirituality Center
St. Charles College
P.O. Drawer C
Grand Coteau, LA 70541-1003
phone: (337) 662-5251 or (337) 662-5252
fax: (337) 662-3187
e-mail: jespirtcen@centurytel.net
Web site: http://home.centurytel.net/spiritualitycenter/

Manresa on the Mississippi
P.O. Box 89, 5858 Louisiana Highway 44
Convent, LA 70723-0089
phone: 225-562-3596 or 800-782-9431
Fax: (225) 562-3147
e-mail: ostini@stargazer.net
Web site: http://bsd.leonce.com/manresa/

Our Lady of the Oaks
214 Church Street
P.O. Drawer D
Grand Coteau, LA 70541
phone: (337) 662-5410

MARYLAND

Loyola Retreat House
9270 Loyola Retreat Road
P.O. Box 9
Faulkner, MD 20632-0009
phone: (301) 870-3515
fax: (301) 392-0808
e-mail: reservations@loyolaretreat.org
Web site: http://www.loyolaretreat.org

MASSACHUSETTS

Campion Renewal Center
319 Concord Road
Weston, MA 02493-1398
phone: (781) 788-6810
fax: (781) 894-5864
e-mail: acopponi@campioncenter.org
Web site: http://www.campioncenter.org

Franciscan Center
459 River Road
Andover, MA 01810
phone: (978) 851-3391
fax: (978) 858-0675
e-mail: FranRetC@aol.com
Web site: http://www.FranRCent.org

Gonzaga Eastern Point Retreat House
37 Niles Pond Road
Gloucester, MA 01830
phone: (978) 283-0013
fax: (978) 282-1989
e-mail: gonzaga@cove.com
Web site: http://www.easternpoint.org/

MICHIGAN

Colombiere Conference Center
9075 Big Lake Road
P.O. Box 139
Clarkston, MI 48347-0139
phone: (248) 620-2534 or (248) 625-5611 ext. 275
fax: (248) 620-2433
e-mail: colombiere@colombiere.com
Web site: http://www.colombiere.com/index.htm

Manresa Jesuit Retreat House
1390 Quarton Road
Bloomfield Hills, MI 48304-3554
phone: (248) 644-4933
fax: (248) 664-8291
e-mail: office@manresa-sj.org
Web site: http://www.manresa-sj.org

MINNESOTA

Jesuit Retreat
8243 Demontreville Trail N
Lake Elmo, MN 55042-9546
phone: (612) 777-1311

Loyola: A Spiritual Renewal Resource
389 N Oxford Street
Saint Paul, MN 55104-4734
phone: (651) 641-0008
e-mail: Staff@LoyolaSRR.org
Web site: http://loyolasrr.org/

MISSOURI

White House Retreat
7400 Christopher Drive
St. Louis, MO 63129
phone: (314) 533-8903 or (800) 643-1003
e-mail: reservations@whretreat.org
Web site: http://whretreat.org/

NEW JERSEY

Loyola Retreat House
161 James Street
Morristown, NJ 07960
phone: (973) 539-0740
fax: (973) 898-9839
e-mail: retreathouse@loyola.org
Web site: http://www.loyola.org

Vincentian Renewal Center
75 Mapleton Road
Princeton, NJ 08540-9614
phone: (609) 520-9626, ext. 4200
fax: (609) 520-0593
e-mail: programs@vincentianfamilycenter.com
Web site: http://www.vincentianfamilycenter.com

Catholic Zen Retreats
Fr. Robert Kennedy, S.J.
phone: (212) 831-5710
e-mail: rocnyc@aol.com

NEW YORK

Bethany Retreat House
202 County Route 105
P.O. Box 1003
Highland Mills, NY 10930-1003
phone: (845) 928-2213
fax: (845) 928-9437
e-mail: bethanyretreat@frontiernet.net
Web site: http://www.rc.net/newyork/bethany

Corazón, at Villa St. Dominic
P.O. Box 189
Glasco, NY 12432
phone: (845) 246-8941
fax: (845) 246-5610
Web site: http://www.sparkill.org/Public/villastdominic.html

Divine Compassion Center for Spiritual Renewal
Sr. Corita Clarke, R.D.C.
52 N Broadway
White Plains, NY 10603-3710
phone: (914) 948-4086
fax: (914) 949-5169
e-mail: dccsr@bestweb.net
Web site: http://www.bestweb.net/~dccsr/

Graymoor Spiritual Life Center
Route 9
P.O. Box 300
Garrison, NY 10524-0330
phone: (845) 424-3641, ext. 3505
e-mail: graymoorcenter@atonementfriars.org
Web site: http://www.atonementfriars.org/page/lifecenter.htm

Linwood Spiritual Center
50 Linwood Road
Rhinebeck, NY 12572-2507
phone: (845) 876-4178 ext. 301
Fax: (845) 876-1920
E-mail: linwood@ulster.net
Web site: http://www.societyofstursula.org/linwood.html

Mount Manresa Jesuit Retreat House
239 Fingerboard Road
Staten Island, NY 10305
phone: (718) 727-3844
fax: (718) 727-4881
e-mail: mountmanresa@si.rr.com
Web site: http://www.manresasi.org/

St. Ignatius Jesuit Retreat House
251 Searingtown Road
Manhasset, NY 11030
phone: (516) 621-8300
fax: (516) 621-7201
e-mail: inisfada@inisfada.net
Web site: http://www.inisfada.net

NORTH CAROLINA

Jesuit House of Prayer
289 NW US 25/70
P.O. Box 7
Hot Springs, NC 28743
Phone/Fax: (828) 622-7366
Email: vpaul@madison.main.nc.us (internet not always available)
Web site: http://www.geocities.com/~jesuit_housenc

OHIO

Jesuit Retreat House of Cleveland
5629 State Road
Parma, OH 44134
phone: (440) 884-9300
fax: (440) 885-1055
e-mail: info@jrh-cleveland.org
Web site: http://www.jrh-cleveland.org

Loyola of the Lakes
700 Killinger Road
Clinton, OH 44216
phone: (330) 896-2315 or (800) 827-1416
fax: (330) 896-0858
e-mail: lotljrh@aol.com
Web site: http://www.loyolaofthelakes.com/loyola/default.shtml

Milford Spiritual Center
5361 S Milford Road
Milford, OH 45150
phone: (513) 248-3500
fax: (513) 248-3503
e-mail: milfordspiritualcenter@zoomtown.com
Web site: http://www.milfordspiritualcenter.org

OREGON

The Jesuit Spirituality Center
424 SW Mill Street
Portland, OR 97286
Phone: (503) 595-1919
Fax: (503) 777-3142
e-mail: sjspirit@aol.com
Web site: http://www.sjspirit.com/

PENNSYLVANIA

Jesuit Center for Spiritual Growth
501 N Church Road
Wernersville, PA 19565-0223
phone: (610) 670-3640
e-mail: jescntbus@talon.net
Web site: http://www.jesuitspiritualcenter.org/

Villa Maria Retreat Center
P.O. Box 424
Villa Maria, PA 16155-0424
phone: (724) 964-8920 ext. 3358
e-mail: CWilpula@humilityofmary.org
Web site: http://villamaria.tripod.com

SOUTH CAROLINA

Springbank Spirituality Center
1345 Springbank Road
Kingstree, SC 29556
phone: (800) 671-0361
fax: (843) 382-5340
e-mail: springbank@mindspring.com
Web site: http://www.springbankspirit.org/

SOUTH DAKOTA

Sioux Spiritual Center
20100 Center Road
Howes, SD 57748-7703
phone: (605) 985-5906
fax: (605) 985-5908
e-mail: ssc@gwtc.net
Web site: http://puffin.creighton.edu/jesuit/ssc/

TEXAS

Montserrat Jesuit Retreat House
P.O. Box 1390
Lake Dallas, TX 75065
phone: (Metro) (940) 321-6020 or (940) 321-6030
fax: (940) 321-6040
e-mail: retreat1@airmail.net
Web site: http://www.montserratretreat.org

WASHINGTON

Ignatian Resource Center
4732 18th Avenue E
Seattle, WA 98112
phone: (206) 329-4824
fax: (206) 726-6179
e-mail: ignatianctr@juno.com

WISCONSIN

Jesuit Retreat House
4800 Fahrnwald Road
Oshkosh, WI 54902
phone: (920) 231-9060
fax: (920) 231-9094
e-mail: office@jesuitretreathouse.org
Web site: http://www.jesuitretreathouse.org

Racine Dominican Retreat Program
Siena Center
5635 Erie Street
Racine, WI 53402-1900
phone: (262) 639-4100
fax: (262) 639-9702
e-mail: rdrp@miliserv.net
Web site: http://www.racinedominicans.org

CANADA

ONTARIO

Loyola House
P.O. Box 245
Guelph, ON N1H 6J9
phone: (519) 824-1250
fax: (519) 767-0994
e-mail: loyola@loyolahouse.ca
Web site: http://www.loyolahouse.ca

Manresa Jesuit Spiritual Renewal Centre
2325 Liverpool Road
Pickering, ON L1X 1V4
phone: (905) 839-2864
fax: (905) 839-7289
e-mail: info@manresa-canada.ca
Web site: http://www.manresa-canada.ca

Martyrs' Shrine
Midland, ON L4R 4K5
phone: (705) 526-3788
fax: (705) 526-1546
e-mail: shrine@csolve.net
Web site: http://www.jesuits.ca/martyrs-shrine/

Mount Carmel Spiritual Centre
7021 Stanley Avenue
Niagara Falls, ON L2G 7B7
phone: (905) 356-4113
fax: (905) 358-2548
e-mail: mtcarmel@computan.on.ca
Web site: http://www.carmelniagara.com